CHESS

The

Easy Way

By

REUBEN FINE

AUTHOR OF

Modern Chess Openings, *Revised Edition*

Basic Chess Endings

CORNERSTONE LIBRARY   NEW YORK

CONTENTS

FOR MY WIFE

in the hope that she'll finally
find out what I am talking about.

INTRODUCTION

"Chess, like music, like love, has the power to make men happy." This memorable phrase of Dr. Tarrasch's has been vehemently seconded and confirmed by the experiences of millions of players extending over a period of fifteen hundred years. In an age like ours, when there is so much leisure time, its pursuit is particularly justified and immensely rewarding.

To the best of our knowledge, chess dates back to the India of the fifth century A.D. Whether it was invented or gradually developed is not clear; most probably the latter. During the Middle Ages traders brought the game to Europe, where it became the most fashionable and respectable pastime of the leisure class. Relics of those bygone days when it was the sport of kings still persist: thus chess is the only game allowed in the House of Parliament.

Kings and their retinues gave way to more modern forms of government and with the democratization of life and the blossoming of civilization the popularity of chess increased in geometrical proportion. By the middle of the nineteenth century chess centers had appeared in every large city on the continent, England and the United States, numerous magazines and newspaper columns devoted exclusively to chess were to be found, congresses with representatives from many different countries were organized.

In modern times chess is normally an integral part of our culture. Many important tournaments, not to mention thousands of minor club affairs, are arranged and widely publicized; great chess experts are occasionally granted state subsidies; literature on all aspects of the game pours forth in an unending stream; expressions such as "gambit," "Pawn," "pieces on the board," have become common currency.

And yet there is a curious bar to the spread of the greatest game in the world: its alleged difficulty. Of course, chess is not ticktacktoe. It is indeed beyond the powers of any mortal to master it completely. But this very complexity is the source of its fascination. For the situations that arise necessarily occupy the complete attention of the player. He cannot think of his business, or of the war, or of his marital woes. Whether he likes it or not, he forgets everything else and concentrates on the peculiar wooden shapes being shifted about on a bare sixty-four squares. And this is why chess is the ideal form of recreation.

But its difficulties have been immensely exaggerated. It is an obvious fact that anybody can learn how to play chess in half an hour. That alone is sufficient to enable him to derive some pleasure from the game.

Naturally, there is more to it than knowing how to move. And it is at this point that the learner's troubles frequently begin. Once the moves have been mastered, further progress is usually haphazard, sketchy, a pure hit-or-miss affair. Many seek guidance in the voluminous literature devoted to the game, but all too often find little or nothing which is directed exclusively at the beginner. Some keep going; others abandon the attempt in the mistaken belief that it is beyond them.

Nevertheless, it is possible to improve at chess and the effort required is by no means exorbitant. The road from the "buzzing, blooming confusion" that the tyro sees at first to the orderly and enjoyable patterns that make chess so charming and intriguing to the more advanced player should, with the help of a good guide, be quickly and easily traversed. This book has been written in order to provide such a guide.

Throughout my intent has been to be systematically fundamental. Everything that is basic has been included; everything unnecessarily complicated or of interest only to experts has been excluded. It is my conviction that the person who masters this work will be able to more than hold his own with the average club player.

The dogmatic approach is essential to secure a proper understanding of the game. Exceptions to the rules will naturally be found, but they are too few to be of importance to any one but an expert.

That few chess books have questions designed to test what has been presented is a defect nurtured by a long tradition. Learning, especially in a game, must involve doing. The problems indicate the extent to which the material has been digested, for they have all occurred in actual games and are typical of those likely to come up again.

If this work succeeds, to however small an extent, in promoting the popularity and development of chess in the English-speaking world, I shall be more than satisfied.

New York, October, 1941.   REUBEN FINE

Chapter I

THE MOVES, RULES AND NOTATION

Chess is played by two opponents on a board of 64 squares, alternately colored White and Black (or light and dark).

The Board and Pieces
Black

White

Technical terms used to describe parts of the board are:

A *file* is a vertical series of squares. There are eight files.

A *rank* is a horizontal series of squares. There are eight ranks.

A *diagonal* is a series of adjacent squares of the same color, going from one edge of the board to the other. There are twenty-six diagonals.

The following diagrams illustrate these terms.

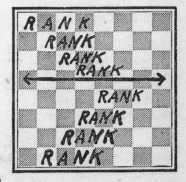

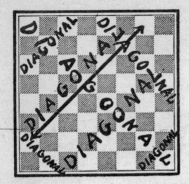 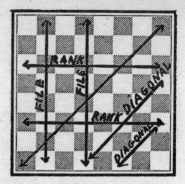

THE PIECES

Each side has sixteen pieces—one King, one Queen, two Rooks, two Bishops, two Knights and eight Pawns.

Since the pieces are also light- and dark-colored, the players are usually referred to as White and Black.

Piece	White	Black
(1) King	♔	♚
(1) Queen	♕	♛
(2) Rooks	♖	♜
(2) Bishops	♗	♝
(2) Knights	♘	♞
(8) Pawns	♙	♟

The initial placement of the board and pieces is shown above. In all diagrams, whether directly indicated or not, the White pieces begin from the bottom, the Black from the top. In actual play the board must always be placed in such a way that each player has a White square on his extreme right. One way to check this is to make sure that each Queen is on her own color, i.e., that the White Queen is on a White square and the Black Queen on a Black square. You wouldn't expect a woman with a white dress to wear black shoes, would you?

HOW THE PIECES MOVE

Moves of the Rook

1. The *Rook* moves any number of squares in one direction on any file or rank, i.e., horizontally or vertically. Thus in the diagram the Rook may play anywhere along the lines indicated by arrows. In this position the Rook can choose one of fourteen squares.

2. The *Bishop* moves any number of squares in one direction on any diagonal. In this diagram the Bishop may be played to any one of thirteen squares.

Moves of the Bishop   Moves of the Queen

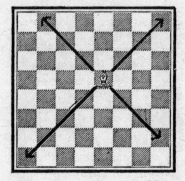 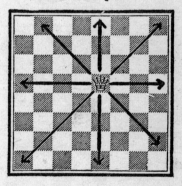

3. The *Queen* moves either as a Bishop or as a Rook, i.e., any number of squares in one direction on any file, rank or diagonal. The diagram shows that there are twenty-seven possible moves with the Queen placed in the center of the board.

4. The *Knight* is halfway between a Bishop and a Rook. It moves one square diagonally in any direction and then one square on a rank or file in the same direction, or vice versa (first rank or file, then diagonal) Thus it may begin as a Bishop and continue as a Rook, or it may begin as a Rook and continue as a Bishop. The diagram illustrates the eight possible moves with the Knight in the center of the

Moves of the Knight

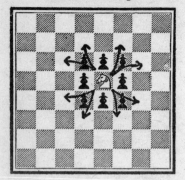

Moves of the Pawn

board. Note that each square can be reached either by making first a Rook move and then a Bishop move or vice versa. Note too that if the condition that the move must continue in the same direction did not exist the Knight could make one move either as a Bishop or as a Rook.

Moves of the King

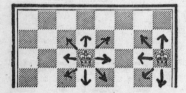

5. The *Pawn* moves directly forward one square at a time, except that in the initial position it may move one or two squares. When the Pawn reaches the eighth rank, it must promote to either a Knight, Bishop, Rook or Queen, regardless of the number of such pieces that happen to be on the board.

Castling "Short" or on the King's Side

Before Castling

After Castling

6. The *King* moves one square in any direction. Its powers are illustrated below. From any square not on the edge of the board it has eight possible plays.

All pieces except the Knight can cross only unoccupied squares. No two pieces may be on the same square at the same time.

Castling "Long" or on the Queen's Side

Before Castling   After Castling

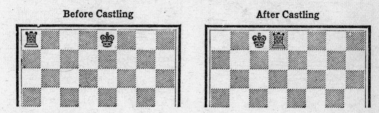

An exception to this exists in the "Castling" privilege. This is a combined move of the King and Rook, but counts as only one move, where first the King, from his original square, is placed two squares either to the right or to the left on the same rank, and then the Rook towards which the King has been moved is placed on the adjacent square on the opposite side of the King. Castling is not permitted (a) if either the King or Rook has been moved previously; (b) if any square between the King and the Rook is occupied by a man; (c) if the King is in check; or (d) if castling would cause the King to pass over or occupy any square on which he would be in check.

Castling with the Rook on the King's side is known as "castling short," with the one on the Queen's side as "castling long." The diagrams give the various positions before and after castling.

CAPTURES

All the pieces except the Pawn capture as they move, merely replacing the enemy man on the square which it had been occupying, and removing that man from the board. Only enemy pieces can be taken. But the King cannot be captured. The Pawn captures diagonally.

Various possibilities are illustrated on page 6.

En passant: A Pawn which has been advanced two squares on its first move is liable to be captured on the following move by the opponent's Pawn that could have captured it if it had moved only one

Bishop captures Rook

Black   Black

Knight captures Pawn

White
Pawn captures
Bishop

White
No captures
are possible

square, precisely as though it had so moved. Thus in the diagram, assuming Black's Pawn has just been played up from its original

Capture en passant
Black

White

square, it may be captured in exactly the same manner as if it had been played up one square. The option of a capture en passant exists for only one move: if it is not exercised at once, it will never again be available.

Check: The King is in "check" if the square he occupies is commanded by an opposing man. When check is announced the King must be removed from check at once. There are three ways of doing this: capturing the checking piece, interposing a piece between the King and the checking piece, and moving the King away. The King must never move into check, nor to any one of the squares adjacent to that occupied by the opposing King. Further, a piece which is so placed between its King and an enemy piece that it screens a check must not be moved in such a way that the King is exposed to check. Such a piece is "pinned."

The diagram illustrates a check and the various methods of getting out of it. Here Black may interpose his own Bishop (1), or he may capture White's Bishop (2), or he may move his King (3). But note that he may not move his King to the square marked with a cross. Nor may Black make any other move, such as checking the White King. That would be "illegal": the move would have to be retracted and a legal one made in its place.

Discovered check occurs when the piece which has just moved does not give check directly, but uncovers one by a piece behind it.

Double check is a position where the enemy King is in check to two different pieces.

Checkmate: The object of the game is to check the enemy King in such a way that there is no escape. This is known as "checkmate" and occurs when none of the three methods of getting out of check is available. The person who is checkmated loses. Some typical checkmates (or mates—the shorter form is frequently used) are shown in the diagrams.

The Three Methods of Getting Out of Check

Black is Checkmated
Black

White

Checkmate   Checkmate

In the first case there is nothing that can be interposed, the Queen cannot be captured because it is defended by the Bishop, while every other square that the Black King could escape to is covered by the White Queen. In the second position Black's flight squares are covered either by the White King or the White Rook, while interposition and capture are both impossible. The third is the most complicated: Black's King has no flight squares, but his Queen can neither interpose nor capture the White Rook only because it is pinned by the White Bishop.

DRAWN GAMES

The game may be won or drawn. It is won by checkmating the opponent, although in contests between strong players it is customary to resign when the preponderance of force is overwhelming.

The game is drawn:

(a) When the player cannot make a legal move and his King is not in check. This King is then said to be stalemated. (STALEMATE)

(b) If the player prove that he can subject the opponent's King to an endlesss series of checks. (PERPETUAL CHECK)

(c) By recurrence of position when the same position occurs three times in the game, and it is the same person's turn to move on each occasion, and if such player claim the draw before the position is altered by further play, otherwise no claim can be sustained. (For the purpose of this clause there shall be no distinction between the King and Queen's Rooks and Knights, or between the original pieces and pieces of the same denomination and color obtained through the promotion of Pawns.) (REPETITION OF POSITION)

(d) By MUTUAL AGREEMENT.

(e) If the player prove that 50 moves have been made on each side without checkmate having been given and without any man having been captured or Pawn moved. (50-MOVE RULE) Exception is made only if it is shown that an ending has resulted where theoretically more than fifty moves are required to give checkmate. In this case a number of moves double the number established by theory as being necessary for this object shall be allowed instead of the 50.

The draw according to this rule must be claimed as soon as the stipulated number of moves has been completed, and will not be allowed at any later period.

GENERAL RULES

1. White plays first and the players then move alternately, one move at a time. A move is obligatory and may not be "passed."

2. The move of a man shall be to an unoccupied square or to a square occupied by an opposing man.

3. The move of a man shall not cause such man to pass over any occupied square, except in the case of the Knight.

4. A legal move of a man to a square occupied by an opposing man requires the removal of that opposing man by the player from the chess board.

5. If an illegal move is made it must be retracted and the game continued as usual. There is no penalty for an illegal move. If in the course of the game it is proved that an illegal move has been made

and not retracted, the position existing immediately before the illegal move was made shall be reinstated and the game shall be continued from that position. If the position cannot be reinstated the game shall be annulled.

NOTATION

Chess players form an international fraternity with a language of their own. This language is a shorthand system to describe the moves made.

First a symbol is attached to each piece. These symbols are the first letters of the names of the pieces, except that Kt is written for Knight to distinguish it from K for King. Thus we have the following letters:

Piece	*Picture*	*Symbol*
King		K
Queen		Q
Rook		R
Bishop		B
Knight		Kt
Pawn		P

The files are given the names of the pieces which occupy the first square on them in the original position. To distinguish the two sides of the board from one another, those pieces nearest the King are known as KR (King's Rook), KKt (King's Knight) and KB (King's Bishop) respectively, while those nearest the Queen are known as QR (Queen's Rook), QKt (Queen's Knight) and QB (Queen's Bishop) respectively, and the files are designated accordingly.

The eight files with their descriptions (identical for White and Black) are shown in the adjoining diagram.

The ranks are numbered from one to eight, each player beginning from his own side, so that "1" for White is "8" for Black. In this way each square has a letter (or two letters) and a number assigned to it uniquely. These are seen in the next diagram. Here we are

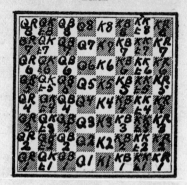

White

looking at the board from the White side. To get Black's "point of view" we need only replace "QR1" by "QR8," "Q2" by "Q7," "KB4" by "KB5" etc. After a little practice the chess board becomes as familiar as the alphabet.

A move is recorded by the letter designating the man moved followed by a dash and the description of the square to which the man has been moved. If any ambiguous interpretation is possible, the square from which the man has been moved is included in parentheses. E.g., if a Knight at K4 goes to Kt5, we write Kt—Kt5, but if there are two Knights, one at K6 and the other at K4, we must write Kt(K4)—Kt5. As a rule, simply "Kt5" is written if there is only one Kt5 to which the piece can go, while "KKt5" or "QKt5" is written if both moves are possible.

Captures are recorded by the letter designated the man capturing, a times sign and the letter designating the man captured. Thus Pawn takes Pawn is written "P×P." Again to avoid ambiguity it may be necessary to include the squares on which one or both pieces are standing. Returning to our illustration above, if White has two Knights at K4 and K6, and Black has two Pawns at KKt4 and QB4 we must write "Kt(K4)×KtP."

It is important to remember that each player records his own moves from his side, but his opponent's moves from his opponent's side. As a result the score sheets must be identical at the close of the game.

The easiest way to familiarize oneself with the English notation is to realize that it is *descriptive* and that the present scoring is merely the end result of a long series of contractions. Thus the earliest recorded games have as the first move "King's Pawn to the fourth square on the King's file," later "King's Pawn to King's fourth square," then "KP to K4," then "P to K4" and finally "P—K4."

Some common abbreviations used are: Castles KR or O—O for Castles K-side; Castles QR or O—O—O for Castles Q-side; ch for check; dis ch for discovered check; dbl ch for double check; mate for checkmate; e.p. for en passant.

As an exercise the reader should play over the first twelve moves of the following game and should reach the position shown in the diagram.

White	*Black*
1 P—K4	P—K4
2 Kt—KB3	Kt—KB3
(Knight to King's Bishop 3)	
3 P—Q4	P×P
(Pawn to Queen's fourth)	(Pawn takes Pawn)
4 P—K5	Kt—K5
(Pawn to King's fifth)	(Knight to King's fifth)
5 Q×P	P—Q4
6 P×P e.p.	Kt×P(Q3)
7 Kt—B3	Kt—B3
8 Q—KB4	B—K2
9 B—Q3	O—O
10 B—K3	B—K3
11 O—O—O	Q—B1
12 KR—K1	B—B3

Black

White

Chapter II

CHECKMATING THE LONE KING

Since the object of the game is to checkmate the opponent, it is of the utmost importance to know what the minimum material required is and how to go about mating.

The minimum force required to administer checkmate (when there is nothing else on the board) is either 1) One Queen, 2) One Rook, 3) Two Bishops or 4) Bishop and Knight. One Bishop or one Knight alone will not do. Surprisingly two Knights will not be able to force the win, although if the opponent makes a mistake he may be mated. However, with one Bishop or one Knight alone no mating position is conceivable.

Before we go on to the details of the procedure it will be helpful to look at checkmate in a somewhat different light. The fundamental positional concept of chess is *mobility*, freedom of movement for the pieces. Checkmate is attacking (checking) the enemy King when his mobility is nil, when he has no legal moves left. Thus there are two elements essential to winning a game: the opposing King has no moves, and he is being attacked. It is not enough to merely reduce his mobility to nil: that would be a stalemate and would result in a draw. Nor is only checking sufficient: true, you make your opponent's life miserable, but you also enable him to prolong his doomed existence.

Since it is always possible to check an exposed King the most difficult job in any mating procedure is to cut down the enemy's mobility. Now we know that a King in the center of the board has eight possible moves, while one on the edge of the board has five, and one in the corner has only three. Consequently our first task is *to drive the enemy King to the edge of the board*. If necessary we will then drive him into the corner.

Next we notice that a piece alone without the aid of the King cannot checkmate. Try it and see! The Queen alone can stalemate, the Rook alone cannot even do that. Similarly two minor pieces alone cannot do the trick. In order to win without the aid of the King it is essential to have at least one piece more than the minimum mating force, e.g., Queen and Bishop, or two Bishops and Knight.

Since we are concerned here only with the mate with the bare essentials the next step after chasing the enemy King back is to bring one's own King up. Once this is done the coup de grace should follow in two or three moves.

These remarks are applicable to all mates, but the execution is different in each case.

1. THE QUEEN

The Queen is the most powerful piece and this mate is consequently easiest.

Before starting out on our mating trip we must first know where we are going, what our final destination is. This goal should be one of two possible mating positions.

First Mating Position
with the Queen.

Second Mating Position
with the Queen.

Now the objectives and methods of the final mating attack are clear to us: White [1] will first drive the Black King to the edge of the board with his Queen, then he will bring his own King up so that the two Kings will be facing one another as shown in the diagrams, and he will finally administer one of the two checkmates. In all this he must above all avoid stalemating the enemy King. And such stalemate is again of one of two types (see diagram). If the enemy King is in the corner always make sure that the Queen is at least three squares away; similarly if the King is in the center see to it that the Queen is on the adjoining rank or file and that the King is at least two ranks away.

Black to Play Is Stalemated.

[1] For the sake of convenience and uniformity the superior side in such endings is invariably referred to as White.

Thus in the first diagram the White Queen should be at K7 (marked with an X), while in the second it should be at KKt7 (also indicated), while the King should be on the sixth rank.

If one remembers these points the elaboration and actual execution of the mate is a relatively simple matter. Let us consider the adjoin-

No. 1

ing diagram (No. 1) as a typical case. The first problem is to drive the King back to the last rank (or file). So we begin with 1 Q—R5, for this confines the Black King to the last three ranks. Then Black replies 1 .... K—B3. Now one may play either the King or the Queen; the most systematic (though not the quickest) method involves using the Queen. Thus 2 Q—Q5, K —K2; 3 Q—B6, K—Q1; 4 Q—Kt7, K—K1. With the King confined to the last rank it would be superfluous to move the Queen again, so the King must be brought up. 5 K— Kt6, K—Q1; 6 K—B6, K—K1; 7 K—Q6, K—B1; 8 K—K6, K—Kt1; 9 K—B6, K—R1; 10 Q—KKt7 mate. Note that if Black had not gone off to hide in the corner he would have been mated much sooner.

2. THE ROOK

This piece is not nearly as strong as the Queen and the mate is accordingly far more difficult. The Rook alone cannot drive the King to the edge of the board—it needs the assistance of its own monarch. Since the Rook is much less powerful than the Queen, there is less danger of stalemate—this is the brighter side of the picture.

Mating Position with the Rook.

In order to mate, the enemy King must again be driven to the edge of the board. The mating position is then the same as the second one with the Queen. Thus the problem here is essentially the same as that in the previous case, the chief difference being that the two preliminary steps (driving the enemy King back

No. 2

and bringing one's own King up) are carried out simultaneously. The only stalemate that should be watched for occurs when the Black King is in the corner.

Starting from any position such as that shown here in No. 2 we would then proceed as follows: 1 R —Q2 (confining the Black King to the right-hand side of the board), 1 .... K—K6; 2 R—Q5, K—K5; 3 K—B5, K—K6; 4 R—Q4 (now he has only three ranks and four files), K—K7; 5 K—Q5, K—K6; 6 K—K5, K—K7; 7 K—K4, K—B7; 8 R—Q3 (see diagram No. 2a), K—K7; 9 K—Q4, K—B7; 10 R—K3, K—Kt7; 11 K—K4, K—B7; 12 K—B4, K—Kt7; 13 R—K2ch, K—B8; 14 K—B3, K—Kt8 (diagram No. 2b); 15 K—Kt3, K—B8; 16 R—K8, K—Kt8; 17 R—K1 mate.

The final maneuver, which involves losing a tempo, or move, should be remembered—it is the key to this mate.

No. 2a

Position after 8 R–Q3.

No. 2b

Position after 14 .... K–Kt8.

3. THE TWO BISHOPS

In the previous cases it has always been sufficient to drive the King to the edge of the board. Here, however, it is essential to have the enemy King in a corner, for though mating positions in the center are possible they cannot be forced. Any corner will do (unlike the case with Bishop and Knight).

The basic mating positions are seen in the diagram. The Bishops alone cannot stalemate, but with the King nearby one misplaced Bishop is enough to throw away a well-earned win. The three possible stalemate positions are illustrated below:

Mating Positions with the Two Bishops.

The mating method is essentially the same as that with a Rook— driving the enemy King back and approaching with one's own King at the same time. The Bishops alone can hold the King off but cannot chase him back.

Black to Play Is Stalemated.

No. 3

Beginning with any arbitrary position (see diagram No. 3) the first task is to reduce the mobility of the Black King. Thus 1 B—B3, K—K6; 2 B—B6, K—Q5. Now that the Bishops are as well placed as possible the King must come up. 3 K—Kt4, K—Q6; 4 B—K5, K—K6; 5 K—B4, K—Q7; 6 B—Q4, K—K7; 7 K—B3, K—B8 (see diagram No. 3a); 8 B—B3, K—K8; 9 B—Kt2, K—K7; 10 B—B5 (a *tempo* move: White cannot approach directly and loses a move to

compel Black to retreat), K—K8; 11 K—Q3, K—Q8 (see diagram No.
3b). From this point on the rest is quite simple: by successively
cutting off the squares to the right of Black he is compelled to play
into the corner. 12 B—Kt4, K—B8; 13 B—KB3, K—Kt7; 14 B—Q1
(the King must not be allowed to escape), K—B8; 15 B—R4, K—Kt8;
16 K—Q2, K—Kt7; 17 K—Q1, K—Kt8; 18 B—B3, K—R7; 19 K—

No. 3a. Position after Black's 7th Move.

No. 3b. Position after Black's 11th Move.

B2, K—R6; 20 B—Kt5, K—R7; 21 B—Kt4, K—R8 (see diagram
No. 3c); 22 B—Q3 (tempo move), K—R7; 23 B—B4ch, K—R8;
24 B—B3 mate.

4. BISHOP AND KNIGHT

This is the hardest case of all because mate can be administered only
in the corner which is of the same
color as the Bishop. If the Black
King wisely retreats to the other
corner more than thirty moves may
be required.

The two mating positions are
seen here.

The curious feature of this
ending is that the Black King
must first be forced into the corner
of the wrong color and then
driven over to the other side
of the board. With best play
this will take nineteen moves,
beginning from diagram No. 4.
Since we must drive Black to

No. 3c. Position after Black's 21st Move.

White to play mates in three moves.

Mating Positions with Bishop and Knight.

No. 4

White to play mates in 19.

the other side of the board (but without letting him escape into the center) the method must consist of successively depriving the Black King of the squares on his left (i.e., the King's side). With this in mind the main variation will go as follows: 1 B—K4, K—B1; 2 B—R7!, K—K1; 3 Kt—K5, K—Q1 (for the alternative 3 .... K—B1 see diagram 4a and discussion); 4 K—K6, K—B2; 5 Kt—Q7, K—Kt2 (or 5 .... K—B3—diagram 4b); 6 B—Q3, K—B3; 7 B—R6, K—B2; 8 B—Kt5, K—Q1; 9 Kt—Kt6, K—B2; 10 Kt—Q5ch, K—Q1; 11 K—Q6, K—B1; 12 K—K7, K—Kt2; 13 K—Q7, K—Kt1; 14 B—R6, K—R2; 15 B—B8, K—Kt1; 16 Kt—K7, K—R2; 17 K—B7, K—R1; 18 B—Kt7ch, K—R2; 19 Kt—B6 mate.

From No. 4a we proceed as follows: 4 Kt—Q7ch, K—K1; 5 K—K6, K—Q1; 6 K—Q6, K—K1; 7 B—Kt6ch, K—Q1; 8 Kt—B5, K—B1; 9 B—K4, K—Q1; 10 B—B6, K—B1; 11 B—Q7ch, K—Kt1; 12 K—B6, K—R2; 13 K—B7, K—R1; 14 B—B8, K—R2; 15 Kt—Q3, K—R1; 16 Kt—K5, K—R2; 17 Kt—B6ch, K—R1; 18 B—Kt7 mate.

In No. 4b it is imperative to prevent the Black King from escaping. Hence we play: 6 B—Q3!, K—Kt2; 7 K—Q6, K—B1; 8 Kt—B5, K—Kt1; 9 K—Q7, K—R2; 10 K—B7, K—R1; 11 K—Kt6, K—Kt1; 12 B—R6, K—R1; 13 B—Kt7ch, K—Kt1; 14 Kt—Q7 mate.

In order to drive the enemy King back to the edge of the board White must make use of two typical positions (see dia-

No. 4a

No. 4b

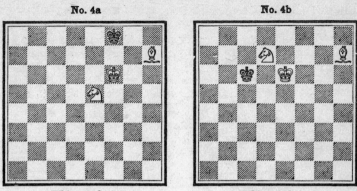

White to play.

White to play.

gram No. 5). In the first—5A—all the points leading towards
the center are inaccessible to the Black King and he cannot maintain the status quo; he must retreat. In the second—5B—
the two pieces are cooperating beautifully. Black's King can
do nothing better than mark time and as soon as the White
King comes up he will have to give way. The important feature
in No. 5B is that the two pieces are diagonally adjacent to one
another, for it is because of this fact that they cover so many
squares.

Starting from some arbitrary position such as No. 6 the most effective continuation would be 1 Kt—B3 (No 5B), K—Q3; 2 B—B6
(No. 5A), K—K3; 3 K—B5, K—K2; 4 K—Q5, K—B1. Black is well
advised to go to the wrong corner, for that is the only way in which he

No. 5. Driving the Black King
Back.

No. 6

can hold out for any appreciable time. 5 K—K6, K—Kt2; 6 Kt—K5, K—B1; 7 K—B6, K—Kt1; 8 Kt—Kt6, K—R2; 9 B—Q5, K—R3; 10 B—Kt8 and now we have position No. 4, since the fact that Black will be chased along the file rather than along the rank makes no difference.

Stalemate positions may be one of three kinds: with the Knight alone, with the Bishop alone, and with both pieces together. All are illustrated here.

Black Is Stalemated.

PROBLEMS

No. 1   No. 2

White to play and mate in two moves.   White to play and mate in three moves.

No. 3

White to play and mate in four moves.

No. 4

White to play and mate in two moves.

No. 5

White to play and mate in three moves.

No. 6

What is the best move?

Chapter III

THE THREE BASIC PRINCIPLES OF CHESS

Two armies are drawn up in battle array. Each has a general, officers, soldiers and a movable citadel. This citadel can be besieged and occupied (in which case the war is won) but not destroyed. It is the center of the drama, the essence of the game.

Nothing more natural then than to go after the King directly. Our first impulse is to pitch in with everything we've got and knock out the opponent, checkmate him. And yet nothing could be more disastrous. For suppose a small detachment of brave soldiers and officers set out to occupy the citadel. What would happen? Both sides have an equal number of men to start with. The citadel will be well defended. The brave attackers will be wiped out or forced to flee ignominiously. Then the enemy, well organized and equipped, will start his own advance. Our own citadel has been shorn of its defenders; it is doomed. A premature attack on a strong enemy position, in chess as in war, is bound to fail.

If a direct frontal attack is sure to be a boomerang, how should we go about defeating the enemy? The only possible answer is that we must undermine the approaches, deprive the enemy of the means to defend himself with, or we must deflect the potential defenders to some other part of the world. In other words we must either capture material or place the enemy pieces in such a position that they will be unable to come to the aid of their King. This will happen if our pieces are more mobile, have more room to move around in.

This then is the theory of chess in the proverbial nutshell. Our first concern is the King. We can only get to the enemy King indirectly, either by capturing material, or by disorganizing his defensive positions. An adequate defense is possible only if the pieces are properly organized and coordinated.

From this discussion we arrive at once at our three fundamental principles—force, mobility, King safety. We may state these as follows:

1. The Principle of Force. The player who is ahead in material should win.

2. *The Principle of Mobility.* The player who has more room for his pieces to move about in has an advantage.

3. *The Principle of Safety.* The safety of the King is of primary importance.

1. THE PRINCIPLE OF FORCE

What reasons are there to validate our first and, in a sense, most basic principle? In the first place we have already demonstrated it to a certain extent in Chapter II. For there we saw that K+Q vs. K, K+B+Kt vs. K, etc., are forced wins, that, when we get to such a point at the end of the game, regardless of how Black plays, he must lose. Similarly we shall see later on that in a large number of cases King and Pawn vs. King is just as easy a win as the mates. How can we extend these findings to all parts of the game? The answer to this is to be found in experience and in the history of the game. By examining the published records, by trying it ourselves, we soon become convinced that with best play an advantage in material, no matter how insignificant, will inevitably lead to checkmate.

To the question, "How much force is required?" we must reply that even one lowly Pawn is enough at the beginning or in the middle of the game. For such a Pawn may always metamorphize into a Queen. Nevertheless, while this is theoretically certain, in practise the exploitation of such a minimal plus presents great difficulties. We shall return to this problem in the chapter on the endings.

At this point the objection may be raised that K+B vs. K is not a win, so that there seem to be cases where the theory falls down. This is, however, true only because we have reached the end of the game. For this stage we must set up the additional proviso that the minimum amount of material essential to win against the lone King is either 1) a Queen, 2) a Rook, 3) 2 Bishops, 4) Bishop and Knight, 5) Pawn, or 6) Bishop (or Knight, or 2 Knights) and Pawn. The first four always lead to checkmate, while the last two are subject to some exceptions.

Since there are six different kinds of pieces it is necessary to set up a table of equivalents in order to be able to know whether an exchange is favorable or not. Again such a table is based partly on the elementary mates (R can mate, B or Kt cannot) and partly on practise. If we take the Pawn as 1 we may set up a table such as this:

Pawn   = 1
Bishop (or
   Knight) = 3
Rook   = 5
Queen   = 9

This is satisfactory for rough calculation but is not as accurate as the following:

Queen is equivalent to	{ Three pieces Plus Pawn or Rook Plus Knight (or B) Plus Pawn
Two Rooks are equivalent to	{ Queen Plus Pawn or Three Minor Pieces
One Rook is equivalent to	{ Bishop or Knight Plus Two Pawns or Five Pawns

Two Minor Pieces are equivalent to Rook Plus Two Pawns
One Piece is equivalent to Three Pawns

A good deal of the beauty of chess derives from combinations where material is sacrificed. Such combinations do not invalidate the theory; on the contrary they most emphatically confirm it. For when the principle is not adhered to there is a specific reason for the deviation. We sacrifice a Pawn to get a bind on the enemy position, or we give up a piece for a mating attack, or we offer the exchange (Rook for a minor piece) to prevent the opponent from castling. In all such cases we recognize the validity of the principle but feel that some greater good may be gained by not sticking to the cut and dried rules.

2. THE PRINCIPLE OF MOBILITY

Our second principle is just as fundamental as the first, but its application is somewhat more complicated. It forms the basis of *strategy* or position play, while force is the leading motive in *tactics* or combinative play. However, just as we saw that force and mobility are both essential for checkmate, as we go on it will become clear that in actual practise the two concepts are inextricably interwoven in all parts of the game.

The evaluation of the pieces is likewise in part shorthand for degree of mobility. Thus if we place the pieces in the center of the board (see Chapter I) we find that the Queen has 27 squares to go to, the Rook 14, Bishop 13, Knight 8 and Pawn 1 (but two captures and promotion potentialities must not be ignored). The longer range of the Bishop is counterbalanced by the greater choice of squares for the Knight, (the B must stick to one color) which is why these two pieces are approximately equal in value. It is well to remember that it is not merely the *number* of squares but also the *kind* that counts. These theoretical considerations would enable us to work out a scale of values independently of actual play, but experience and practise are a simpler guide.

The greater mobility which an extra piece affords is obvious. It is not so clear that more mobility may often be so effective that it will yield an advantage in force. Yet throughout the game questions of mobility are paramount. We shall confine ourselves to a few striking examples here because this point will be illustrated so frequently in the later chapters.

The place where the applications are most obvious is in Pawn play, for the Pawns are relatively fixed. Precisely because the Pawn has so few moves to begin with it is necessary not to reduce this number still further. Thus in No. 7 we find that 6 Pawns cannot win against the lone White King because they are all on one file. Place any Black Pawn on any other square on the board, thus giving it a move, and the win is child's play. For that matter give one single Pawn plenty of leeway and it will be superior to this paralyzed sextuplet. Thus in No. 8 the King can help the Pawn to promote: 1 .... K—K6;

No. 7

Draw.

2 K—K1, P—Q6; 3 K—Q1, P—Q7; 4 K—B2, K—K7; 5 K—B3, P—Q8 = Q etc.

No 8.

Black wins.

No. 9

White wins. Draw if the Black QRP is at QR3 instead of QR4.

A number of Pawns on one file, i.e., "doubled" (two) or "tripled" Pawns, are weak, precisely because they have so few moves at their disposal.

Next to having Pawns doubled the worst thing that can happen is to have them blocked. In No. 9 we see this quite plainly. Here White has a simple win: he goes over to the Q-side, captures both Pawns and then queens the QRP. Meanwhile the Black King must lose valuable time to capture the KRP. Thus: 1 K—Q4, K—B4; 2 K—B4, K—Kt5; 3 K—Kt5, K—R6; 4 K×KtP, K×P; 5 K×P, K—Kt6; 6 K—Kt6, K—B5; 7 P—R5, K—K4; 8 P—R6, K—Q3; 9 P—R7, K—Q2; 10 P—

No. 10

Black wins because White's Rook has no mobility.

R8 = Q etc. Now place the Black QRP at QR3, leaving the other pieces and Pawns unchanged. Then the QKtP has a move and the situation is radically different, for now the two Pawns can put up a fight: 1 K—Q4, K—B4; 2 K—Q5, K—Kt5; 3 K—B6, P—Kt4! (before this would have been meaningless). If White should now exchange Pawns Black's King will capture the last remaining Pawn and the game will be drawn. But should White try to hold on to his last Pawn he will lose: 4 P—R5?, P—Kt5; 5 K—Kt6, P—Kt6; 6 K×P, P—Kt7; 7 K—R7, P—Kt8 = Q and

the Queen will win easily (for this ending see Chapter VII).

Examples with pieces also abound. In No. 10 White would have an easy win with his Rook out in the open. But now he loses because his Rook is stuck and has no way out of the trap.

Again in No. 11 a Pawn is stronger than a Knight because it queens by force. Wherever the Kt goes, P—R7—R8 = Q cannot be prevented. But with the Kt at R2, stopping the Pawn, Black wins without much trouble.

We see then that mobility may even in exceptional cases reverse our accepted value equivalents. Such possibilities are unusual but should always be taken into consideration.

The reader will doubtless have noticed that our second principle is less emphatic than our first. Force *wins*, but *mobility* merely confers an *advantage*. The reason for this is twofold. In the first place the rules of chess create an unavoidable margin between a superior position and one which leads to checkmate. With a Pawn, or (without Pawns) a piece, to the good at the end of the game there are many cases where no win is possible because the best that can be done is to stalemate the opponent. This is why we must always be make sure that we shall have sufficient material left at the end of the game, and why we must not exchange Pawns and pieces heedlessly. In the second place greater mobility is often only temporary in character. E.g., in No.

10, if White's King had time to capture the Black QKtP, the White Rook would be freed and Black's superiority dissipated. Or in No. 11 if the White King were at K3, Black could play 1 .... Kt—Q3 and after 2 P—R7, Kt—B5ch; 3 K—Q 4, Kt—Kt3 stop the Pawn and hold the position. It is due to this fact that a superiority in mobility must be utilized more energetically than one in force.

No. 11

A simple corollary of our mobility theory is the *Principle of Cooperation*. The pieces must not duplicate one another's activities, but must work together towards a common goal. For it is only in this way that they attain their maximum mobility, which is equivalent to their maximum effectiveness.

White wins. Black would win if his Kt were at R2, blockading the Pawn.

Thus in No. 12 the Knights are in one another's hair. There is a weak Pawn at Black's K3: if both could attack it, it would fall. So

No. 12

White wins as soon as his Knights cooperate in the attack on the Black KP.

No. 13

White to play wins.

we play 1 Kt—K1, R—K1; 2 Kt(K1)—Q3, K—K2; 3 Kt—B5, K— B2; 4 Kt(B4)×P, R×Kt; 5 Kt×R, K×Kt; 6 P—Q5ch, P×Pch; 7 K—Q4, K—Q2; 8 K×P, K—K2; 9 P—K6 and wins quickly: 9 .... K—K1; 10 K—Q6, K—Q1; 11 P—K7ch, K—K1; 12 K—K6, P—Kt3; 13 P—R6!, P—Kt4; 14 P—R7, P—Kt5; 15 P—R8=Q mate.

Again in No. 13 Black's pieces are sadly disunited: his Rook sulks gloomily in a corner, his Knight is shelved, his Queen stares into space on the other side of the board, his King is deserted and disconsolate. Small wonder that he can be mated by the White Queen and Knight which work together in perfect harmony: 1 Kt—B7ch, K—Kt1; 2 Kt—R6 dbl ch, K—R1; 3 Q—Kt8ch!, R×Q; 4 Kt—B7 mate. This is known as Philidor's Legacy.

3. THE PRINCIPLE OF SAFETY

This too is in every sense fundamental, for if it is violated immediate loss of the game may result. It is applicable chiefly in the opening and middle game. To put it differently, unless there are only a few pieces left on the board one must see to it that the King is not exposed to a dangerous attack which might lead to mate or to serious material loss.

No. 14

Black to play cannot avoid mate.

The best way to defend the King is not to move the Pawns in his neighborhood. As a rule it is practically impossible to attack a King which is surrounded by Pawns on their original squares.

No. 14 is a striking illustration of our principle. White has three mating threats: Q—Kt7 mate, Q —R6 mate and R—R1ch, Q—R5; R×Q mate. Not more than two of these can be forestalled by one Black move. E.g., 1 .... R—B2; 2 R—R1ch, R—R2; 3 Q×R mate.

Chapter IV

THE OPENING

PART I

TEN FUNDAMENTAL RULES

There is a form of the game, quite common in India, where both sides start off by making as many moves as they care to, paying no attention whatsoever to what their opponents do. The only restriction is that no piece may go beyond the fourth rank. When the players are satisfied that their opening positions cannot be improved upon they call a halt and continue in the regulation manner.

It would be wonderful if we were allowed to enjoy the same amount of freedom. Then our plans could never miscarry, our threats could never be parried, our combinations could never be refuted.

But in our modern chess you must constantly be thinking of your opponent. "If I go here and then here, he will counter with that and I'm busted." (A technical term in common use—it is equivalent to "lost.") You do not play in a vacuum; there is plenty of air around during a game, some cold and some not so cold. You don't, or at least you shouldn't, make a move without first considering what the reply will be.

This then is the first and in a sense most central point that you should bear in mind throughout the game as a whole and in the opening in particular. Associate every move which you intend making with its probable consequences.

Let us apply this to the most fundamental idea in the opening— *development*. *Development* is a technical term which means simply getting your pieces into play. A piece is *developed* if it is off its original square. But development is not an abstract mathematical exercise; it is closely influenced by the maneuver of the fellow across the board. As a result time is of the essence. You must develop quickly or not at all.

It does not require much argument to show that if your opponent were asleep or had some other good reason for not moving, you could build up a winning position in precious few moves. E.g., if you were

allowed to go anywhere and keep on moving, you could force mate in
four moves. (1 P—K4, 2 B—B4, 3 Q—B3 and 4 Q×BP, or 4 B×BP
mate. This is often called the Scholar's Mate.) Even if you were
limited to the first four ranks, you could force an overwhelming position quickly. Make sixteen moves, and you can maneuver in such a
way that mate in two is unavoidable. (Odds of "Make as many
moves as you like" are occasionally given, even to strong players, so
that the best continuation is worth reproduction here: 1 P—Q4, 2 Q—
Q2, 3 Q—B4, 4 Kt—Q2, 5 Kt—B4, 6 Kt—B3, 7 Kt(B3)—Q2, 8 Kt—
K4, 9 P—QR4, 10 R—R3, 11 R—K3, 12 P—R4, 13 R(R1)—R3,
14 R(R3)—B3, 15 P—KKt3, 16 B—R3. See diagram below.)

Black to play cannot prevent mate in
two moves.

The pieces have few or no moves; the
problem is to get them out.

Still, normally your opponent does not have his hands tied behind
his back so that Scholar's Mates and similar extravaganzas are out of
the question against any sort of reasonable defense. If, e.g., after
1 P—K4, P—K4; 2 B—B4, Kt—KB3; you persist in trying 3 Q—B3
in the hope that your opponent will remove his Knight and allow
mate you are apt to find yourself sadly disappointed and your Queen
badly misplaced, while if you play 3 Q—R5, exultantly preparing
4 Q×P mate, the Queen will be removed with gusto. The conclusion
that is worth emphasis is that normally an early mate is a pleasant
but impossible dream, and that any attempt to force it will be suicide.
If he does not make a gross blunder, even a beginner could hold out for
twenty-five moves against the world champion.

After these preliminaries we can come back to the basic question:
What should you aim for in the opening? To answer this we must
examine the opening position. You have already seen that one of the
two fundamental concepts in all aspects of the game is freedom or
mobility. When play starts, only the Knights can move. The King,

Queen, both Rooks and both Bishops are stalemated. The Rooks, which normally should work together, are far apart and cannot even offer one another moral support. Worst of all, the King is muzzled and tied down to the center of the board, where he is an easy target.

From our Principle of Mobility we can conclude that it is essential to provide adequate elbow room for the pieces—to develop them—, while the Principle of Safety tells us that we must get the King out of the danger zone.

So our first job is to loosen the straitjacket: to get the pieces out to develop them. Still, this alone is not enough. *The chief strategic objective in the opening is the most effective and harmonious development of all the pieces.* Just how this should be done will be brought out in detail in this chapter. But it is well to keep this thought in mind throughout: we are not interested in one Knight or one Bishop or the Queen or even the King, but in their sum total, *the position as a whole.* The analogy with a modern army is almost perfect: chess is totalitarian war, although fortunately a much more palatable variant than the real thing.

FIRST RULE: OPEN WITH EITHER THE KING'S PAWN OR THE QUEEN'S PAWN.

Your immediate object is to get some breathing space for your pieces. By playing out one of the center Pawns you free the Queen and a Bishop. Any other beginning is a waste of time, for it helps to develop at most only a single piece.

Black does best to copy White's first move. The irregular (i.e., other than 1 .... P—K4 or 1 .... P—Q4) defences to both King Pawn and Queen Pawn openings are full of complicated pitfalls and should not be attempted by an inexperienced player.

Play your Pawn up two squares. This is an advisable policy under any circumstances, but to fail to do so with a center Pawn at the start is tantamount to making your opponent a present of a move.

Let us assume that the game has opened with 1 P—K4, P—K4. Both sides can now develop KKt, KB and KR without any further Pawn moves, but the QP bars the way for the Q-side pieces. In what order should the pieces now be brought into play? This question leads us to consider some more basic principles. Experience has demonstrated time and again that the first player has slightly the better of it. As a great optimist once put it: "When I'm White I win because I'm White; when I'm Black I win because I'm Bogoljuboff." Now, this advantage, in view of the symmetry of the beginning position, consists solely of what is called the initiative—White calls the tune and Black has to dance to it. In our terms White has greater initial mobility. Of course, this fact does not mean that Black must lose or has a bad game—the second player will always have a good deal of leeway. It does mean, however, that any deviation from sound opening principles on Black's part will meet much more drastic punishment than a corresponding lapse by his opponent.

Mobility, unlike force, is a temporary advantage. A few weak moves and it is gone. To preserve it, to capitalize upon it, you must proceed energetically. And energy, on the chess board, consists of *threats*. If Black is constantly preoccupied with the problem of defending weak points, he will never have time to develop his pieces harmoniously. Forced to respond, not to the normal exigencies of his position, but to the demands made upon it by his opponent, he will have to twist and turn and squirm to be able to continue playing at all. Eventually either his patience or the good moves at his disposal or both will wear out, and he will lose material or be mated. Then the advantage in mobility, which is short-lived and by no means necessarily decisive, is transformed into one of force which requires only time to be converted into a win. This gives us our

SECOND RULE: WHEREVER POSSIBLE, MAKE A GOOD DEVELOPING MOVE WHICH THREATENS SOMETHING.

But threats alone are not sufficient: they must fit in with the general pattern of correct development. If after 1 P—K4, P—K4 you play 2 Q—R5? you threaten 3 Q×Pch, but on 2 .... Kt—QB3; 3 Kt—KB3, Kt—B3 your Queen must move again and you lose valuable time. I.e., you must play your Queen again and your opponent will get ahead of you in development. This accounts for the qualification "good" in our rule. The piece which is most ideally suited for attack in the early stages is the Knight. Hence our

THIRD RULE: DEVELOP KNIGHTS BEFORE BISHOPS.

Let us look at the position after 1 P—K4, P—K4 again to see how these rules will work out. If White makes some non-committal move, say 2 P—Q3, Black replies 2 .... P—Q4; 3 Kt—QB3, P×P and now he has the initiative. If a B develops, say, 2 B—Kt5, then 2 .... Kt—KB3; 3 Kt—QB3, P—B3; 4 B—R4, B—B4 again solves Black's opening problem: his pieces are out and working together well. Again, if White develops the Queen's Knight (2 Kt—QB3) Black again has a wide variety of moves and can get a good game in a number of ways. Thus by elimination we get to *2 Kt—KB3* as best. For this is the only normal developing move which involves a threat (3 Kt×P).

The strongest square for a Knight is in the center (K5, Q5, K4, Q4), and the best initial move with a Knight is Kt—B3. This follows immediately from the Principle of Mobility. For from any center square the Knight has eight possible moves, and every point that it covers is important. Place it on Kt3, and it will have only six moves, on R3 only four, on R1, only two. B3 is the quickest, most convenient approach to the center.

Does this mean that one is to play the Knight to K5 or Q5 directly? Most emphatically no! In the first place it will be driven away immediately. But perhaps more important is the fact that we would thereby be neglecting the other pieces. All our forces must cooperate. We must have no pampered pets. With every move the welfare of the whole, not merely of one single unit, must be considered. This brings us to our

FOURTH RULE: PICK THE MOST SUITABLE SQUARE FOR A PIECE AND DEVELOP IT THERE ONCE AND FOR ALL.

This is by far the most comprehensive rule of all, and it accordingly merits a good deal of elaboration.

The most suitable square for a piece is one where it does something (either constructive or preventive) and is not subject to a harmful attack. This means that the most effective placement will vary with the Pawn skeleton and with the positions of the other pieces.

We have already noted that a Knight should go to B3. In some cases (especially when one is trying to set up a center with Pawns at K4 and Q4) it may be advisable to play one Knight to Q2 or K2 in order to free the BP, but this is the only real exception to our rule.

A Bishop is most effective when it is pinning a Knight, for in that way it creates a bind on the enemy position. E.g., in the Queen's Gambit, after 1 P—Q4, P—Q4; 2 P—QB4, P—K3; 3 Kt—QB3, Kt—KB3; *4 B—Kt5* is best because it limits the mobility of the Black Knight and Queen. In line with this theory, the Black Bishop should strive to release the pin, i.e., play 4 .... B—K2 and prepare to remove the Knight at an appropriate moment.

It is bad policy to place the Bishop on a square from which he is bound to be driven by a Pawn. E.g., in the French Defense 1 P—K4, P—K3, the move 2 B—B4? is weak because the natural reply 2 .... P—Q4 compels it to make some other move and thus lose time.

As the game progresses one is faced by the problem of where to put the Rooks. In general it is best to have one on each of the center files (K and Q). Where there is an *open file* (one with no Pawns on it) the Rook should occupy it at the earliest possible moment.

The Queen should be kept in the background until all or most of the other pieces are out.

A few important warnings:

Don't move a piece twice in the opening.

Don't exchange a piece that is developed for one that is not developed.

Don't exchange without good reason.

Don't block the path of development of your pieces.

Don't block either center Pawn.

The last "Don't" suggests an examination of Pawn play. No mistake is more often repeated with frightful results than unnecessary Pawn moves. This is especially true of the opening, where a useless Pawn move costs valuable time which should have been used for the development of a piece. Hence our

FIFTH RULE: MAKE ONE OR TWO PAWN MOVES IN THE OPENING, NOT MORE.

Besides losing time, more Pawn moves inevitably create weaknesses. Sometimes these weaknesses are infinitesimal and even a master could not exploit them properly. But often they prevent a rapid and harmonious set-up of the pieces.

This point is particularly applicable to the Pawns which guard the King (chiefly the KBP, to a lesser extent the KKtP and KRP). In the KP openings it is always a mistake for Black to move his KBP at an early stage. E.g., if after 1 P—K4, P—K4; 2 Kt—KB3, Black defends his KP by 2 .... P—KB3? the weakening of his King position (violation of our third principle) is fatal. White wins by 3 Kt×P!, P×Kt; 4 Q—R5ch, P—Kt3; 5 Q×KPch, Q—K2; 6 Q×R, Kt—KB3; 7 Kt—B3, P—Q3; 8 P—Q4 etc.,—the Queen will eventually escape.

But even if this sacrifice were not possible the weakening of the King-protecting Pawn covering is a grave positional handicap. Suppose Black defended himself as follows: 1 P—K4, P—K4; 2 Kt—KB3, Kt—QB3; 3 B—B4, P—B3? Now the sacrifice 4 Kt×P?, Kt×Kt is incorrect, i.e., Black will win. Still, White can play 4 P—Q4, P—Q3; 5 O—O, B—K2; 6 P—B3 and achieve a healthy, free development, while Black has not only deprived his KKt of its best square but also prevented his King from castling.

Two cute illustrations of the dangers inherent in a move of any Pawn near the King help to impress this point.

1 P—Q4, Kt—KB3; 2 P—QR3?, P—K3; 3 Kt—Q2, Kt—Kt5; 4 P—R3??, Kt—K6; and to avoid losing his Queen White must reply 5 P×Kt, when 5 .... Q—R5ch; 6 P—Kt3, Q×Pch is mate.—The shortest tournament game on record.

1 P—Q4, P—K3; 2 P—QB4, P—QB3?; 3 Kt—QB3, Kt—K2?; 4 Kt—K4, P—KB4??; 5 Kt—Q6 mate.

The Queen is such a powerful piece that one is sorely tempted to produce all kinds of mating or other threats with her help, in the hope that one may succeed. This hope is invariably illusory and is bound to be shattered against the rocks of a correct defense. It could not be otherwise, for moving the Queen often in the early part of the game is a violation of the principle of cooperation. The Queen alone can do little or nothing without the aid of the other pieces. Yet, because this mistake is made so often, we include the

SIXTH RULE: DO NOT BRING YOUR QUEEN OUT EARLY.

We repeat: to do so loses valuable time and hinders the development of the other pieces. The Queen should not stick her pretty neck out: it is worth too much.

The rules given thus far are adequate for the first four or five moves, i.e., the purely developmental stage of the opening. Nevertheless we know that there is more to it than this. The problem of the opening is threefold: to develop the pieces, to safeguard the King, and to gain control or at least equality in the center. With the first six rules all questions concerning development alone can be answered.

The safety of the King is secured by removing it to one side of the board. While this may seem a bit strange, there are two perfectly simple reasons for it. Defense of the monarch is based on a mobile and well-organized army. If all the pieces are working together properly an attack against the King is bound to fail. But the King in the center obstructs the free cooperation of all the pieces. The Rooks cannot support one another, open files cannot be occupied, the best square for a piece may be unavailable, because it is needed for the protection of the King. Then too the King in the center is exposed to attacks from two sides, while once it is off in the corner there is only one avenue of approach. A particularly important result of this double exposure is that it becomes dangerous to move Pawns. For, as we have seen, the Principle of Safety makes it imperative not to touch any of the Pawns near the King. If the Pawns are advanced recklessly there will no longer be any safe spot on the board. The King will constantly have to worry about annoying pursuers, something which should ordinarily not be the case.

A subsidiary reason is that the square KB2 is the Achilles' heel of the position, especially for Black. Innumerable combinations beginning with a sacrifice or capture at KB7 culminate in an orgy of brilliancy; no method of punishment of incorrect opening play is so effective as an attack against that weak point. This is to be expected, for at the beginning of the game that square is the only one defended only by the King and not by a piece. Enough has been said to show the need for our

SEVENTH RULE: CASTLE AS SOON AS POSSIBLE, PREFERABLY ON THE KING'S SIDE.

The reason for the qualification that the K-side is a safer haven than the Q-side is that experience has shown that any attack against the King is always easier to carry out on the Q-side than on the other wing. Castling is, of course, the most effective means of getting the King into the corner because it develops the Rook at the same time.

We have made many allusions to the importance of the center; now we must elaborate the theory systematically. Despite the fact that this theory has been the subject of many a caustic dispute between eminent masters, it is really as simple as ABC. Everything is based upon our

EIGHTH RULE: PLAY TO GET CONTROL OF THE CENTER.

This must necessarily remain in such a general form, although many specific additions will be made in the course of the discussion. The whole theory is most easily explained by answering four questions: What the center is, why it is valuable, what control is, and how one can get control.

Shaded Area Is the Center.

Dotted area is the subsidiary center. One should try to place Kt's in the center, and B's in the subsidiary center.

1. What is the center? The center consists of the four squares in the middle of the board: K4, Q4, K5, Q5. In addition the approaches may be called the subsidiary center —this consists of all the squares touching the center directly.

2. What is the value of the center? The center is the region of greatest mobility. Place a Knight at R1; it can go to two squares. Place it at K5; it can go to eight. Place a Queen at R1: it has 21 possible moves. Place it at K5: it has 27. And so on down the line: every piece is most effective in the center.

The pieces are not static chunks of wood: they are units designed to strike at the enemy defenses. Chessic blitzkrieg demands speed, mobility. We shift a piece into high gear by placing it in the center. And just as in real blitzkrieg the first objective is to seize the railroad terminals and airports in order to augment the striking power of our forces, so in its chessic equivalent we secure the center in order to be able to shift the pieces around more swiftly and more effectively.

There is another essential point in which the analogy holds. By occupying a strategic railroad terminal an army prevents the enemy from uniting his forces. The same thing results on the chess board. And in both cases the disruption and isolation of enemy forces make their destruction easier.

There is still a third respect in which control of the center is beneficial. The amount of terrain on the board is strictly limited: 64

measly squares. Usually each side controls the four ranks nearest to it. If to this is added one or two central squares, part of the enemy territory is occupied and the mobility of his pieces is considerably reduced.

To sum up: the value of the center is that 1) pieces placed in it attain maximum mobility; 2) the opponent's pieces are disunited; 3) one gains control of more space than the opponent.

3. *What is meant by control of the center?* This has proved to be a bone of contention because control and occupation have often been confused.

By control we mean simply the ability to place pieces on a vital central square without having them captured and to capture any enemy piece which goes to that square. E.g., after 1 P—K4, P—K4, each side has control of his Q5 square, although this control is not permanent because the advance of the QP has not yet clarified the situation.

Pawn skeleton in favor of White because he controls a more advanced center square.

It is more important to be able to occupy the more advanced center square (your own K5 or Q5) because you thereby automatically secure more space. This is why a Pawn skeleton with White's Pawn at K4 vs. Black's Pawn at Q3 is in favor of White: the square that he controls is more important. We must distinguish control by the various pieces and control by Pawns (though they frequently go together).

Unless there are immediate effective threats on both sides of the board the Bishop should control the center from a distance, rather than occupy it. The Bishop is a long-range piece: it can attack equally well whether it is six squares away or one.

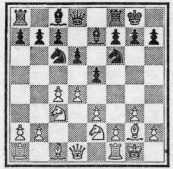

No. 15

White has control of Q5. If necessary he should occupy it with a Knight.

Thus in No. 15 we do not enhance the value of the B, by playing B—Q5, but Kt—Q5 would increase the power of the Kt.

The Kt should attempt to occupy a central square, for it is of little use at a distance. It may safely be assumed that a Kt strongly entrenched at K5 or Q5 (i.e., so that it cannot be driven away) is half a Pawn stronger than a Kt in some weaker position. This means, e.g., that it will as a rule be advisable to sacrifice a Rook for Knight and Pawn if one can also place one's own Kt in an impregnable center position.

A Rook helps to control the center by occupying an open file.

Pawn play in the center is somewhat different. First of all, if one side has one Pawn in the center and the other none he has a slight advantage. (This has already been noted.) The all-important implication of this fact is that a Pawn at K4 vs. one at Q3, or at Q4 vs. one at K3 confers a small superiority. But Pawn at K4 vs. one at K3, while likewise advantageous because it helps to control more terrain, is not a true example of control of the center because the square Q5 cannot be occupied.

In the second place two Pawns in the center vs. none represent a marked advantage.

And finally, two Pawns in the center vs. one are about the same as one vs. none.

4. How can one get control of the center? The answer to this is quite simple from a theoretical point of view: by playing up both center Pawns as soon as convenient. However, since chess is a game which should be drawn with perfect play by both sides, control which confers a marked advantage is possible only if the opponent plays weakly. If control is not feasible (this is especially important for Black) one should at least secure equality.

The method should be guided by the

NINTH RULE: ALWAYS TRY TO MAINTAIN AT LEAST ONE PAWN IN THE CENTER.

This is a convenient guide which will enable one to avoid many opening pitfalls and understand the ideas behind many seemingly obscure opening variations.

We have already noted that a center Pawn is superior to one not in the center, that, e.g., the Pawn position K4 vs. Q3 is better for White. Consequently if Black follows the rule he will avoid any such Pawn configuration.

A corollary of our rule is that one must get rid of the opponent's center Pawns whenever and wherever possible. This is the only way in which one can avoid the inferior Pawn skeleton. An important application of this fact in KP openings is seen in No. 16. The strongest move for Black is 4 .... Kt×P (beginning: 1 P—K4, P—K4; 2 Kt—KB3, Kt—QB3; 3 Kt—B3, Kt—B3; 4 B—B4). If then 5 B×Pch?,

K×B; 6 Kt×Kt, P—Q4! the temporary displacement of the King is meaningless in view of the powerful Pawn phalanx in the center. Best play is 5 Kt×Kt, P—Q4; 6 B—Q3, P×Kt; 7 B×P, B—Q3; when White just manages to get an even game by 8 P—Q4.

This stratagem to remove the opponent's KP is quite common in these openings and should always be watched for.

The subsidiary center Pawns (bordering the center) should be maneuvered to aid the center Pawns. I.e., if there is a threat of capturing a center Pawn, a subsidiary Pawn should be there to take its place. More concretely, if White has Pawns at K4 and Q4, Black at K4, White should have a Pawn at QB3 to recapture, while Black should have one at Q3. It is only when no such reserves are available that an exchange of a center Pawn is of any value.

No. 16

Black should play 4 …. Kt×P.

Another consequence of this rule is the maxim: capture towards the center. While this may at times seem to have only a remote connection with the actual center, it will always have great value. One important and typical example is seen in No. 17. (Preliminary moves: 1 P—K4, P—K4; 2 Kt—KB3, Kt—QB3; 3 B—B4, B—B4; 4 Kt—B3, Kt—B3; 5 P—Q3, P—Q3; 6 O—O, O—O; 7 Kt—QR4, B—QKt5; 8 P—B3, B—R4; 9 P—QKt4, B—Kt3.) On 10 Kt×B it is essential to recapture with the RP: 10 …. RP×KT For by doing so Black opens the R file for his Rook and also keeps an eventual support for a Pawn at Q4 (…. P—QB3 and …. P—Q4). 10 …. BP×KT? would not only yield the square Q4 irretrievably, but would also split the Pawns into two disconnected groups.

No. 17

On Kt×B, RP (and not BP) should recapture.

Finally we must consider the question of a pure Pawn center.

To have Pawns at K4 and Q4 is an advantage, other things being equal, and every effort should be made to maintain them there. It follows that once you have played 1 P—K4, securing P—Q4 under satisfactory circumstances is a major strategical goal, and similarly after 1 P—Q4, you should attempt to get P—K4 in.

While the line of demarcation between opening and middle game is somewhat arbitrary we know that the characteristic feature of the opening is development, while that of the middle game is attack. We also know that attacks in the opening are sometimes premature, but often diabolically effective. This is why chess players are divided into two schools, the Sacrificers and the Acceptors. The Sacrificers believe in reckless courage, limitless daring, casting caution to the winds, in the hope that luck will favor the brave and they will produce an immortal masterpiece. They always refer to their opponents as unimaginative wood shifters. The Acceptors scorn anything but inexorable logic, prefer to play safe, accept every sacrifice offered them and rely on the magical powers of defense. The great hero of the Sacrificers is Morphy (who was known to his own generation as the dullest player alive); the idol of the Acceptors is Steinitz (who has produced some of the most brilliant chess on record). Sometimes the Sacrificers are known as the Latin school, or those gifted with the Latin temperament, doubtless because most of its devotees have been Slavs. For an equally good reason the Acceptors are often called the German school, since most of its exponents are Englishmen. But before taking sides in this endless dispute the man who is most interested in putting up a good game of chess will do well to adhere to the

TENTH RULE: DO NOT SACRIFICE WITHOUT A CLEAR AND ADEQUATE REASON.

To be able to apply this rule we must specify the acceptable reasons. For a sacrifice is a violation of the Principle of Force and can accordingly be correct only under special circumstances. It should be remembered that in the following discussion we are confining ourselves to sacrifices in the openings.

The sacrifice of a piece or more must result in a strong attack against the enemy King. Purely positional considerations which do not affect the King are sure to be inadequate. E.g., a gambit occasionally seen is 1 P—K4, P—K4; 2 Kt—KB3, Kt—QB3; 3 Kt×P?, Kt×Kt; 4 P—Q4. We know that Black will soon be able to castle and that consequently a direct attack on the King is unthinkable. So we reject the whole conception as theoretically unsound. But in the "Fried Liver" Attack, 1 P—K4, P—K4; 2 Kt—KB3, Kt—QB3; 3 B—B4, Kt—B3; 4 Kt—Kt5, P—Q4; 5 P×P, Kt×P; 6 Kt×BP, K×Kt; 7 Q—B3ch, K—K3; 8 Kt—B3, Kt(B3)—Kt5; 9 Q—K4 the Black King is out in the open and there is no telling what will happen. So we can safely assume that this combination deserves further analysis.

To give up two Pawns one should likewise secure a strong attack against the King, but a great advantage in development may on occasion do. Thus in the Danish Gambit, 1 P—K4, P—K4; 2 P—Q4, P×P; 3 P—QB3, P×P; 4 B—QB4, P×P; 5 B×KtP, White will soon have all his pieces adequately placed, while Black will have a hard job getting his into play.

The most common and therefore most important is the offer of one Pawn. For such a sacrifice there must be one of four reasons:

1. Secure a tangible advantage in development.
2. Deflect the enemy Queen.
3. Prevent the opponent from castling, either permanently, or temporarily (two or three moves).
4. Build up a strong attack.

No. 18

White has sacrificed a Pawn for three tempi.

Usually several of these will go together, but this division will nevertheless be found to be of great practical value.

An advantage in development must consist of at least three tempi (moves) or lead to a permanently cramped position. A typical case is seen in No. 18 (Game Alekhine-Flohr, Nottingham, 1936). The opening moves were: 1 P—K4, P—K3; 2 P—Q4, P—Q4; 3 Kt—QB3, B—Kt5; 4 B—Q2, P×P; 5 Kt×P, Q×P; 6 B—Q3, B×Bch; 7 Q×B, Q—Q1?; 8 O—O—O, Q—K2; 9 Kt—KB3. Here White has five pieces developed to his opponent's one (and that the Queen!), so that it is reasonable to suppose that his position is worth a Pawn. Black, of course, should have captured the QKtP on his 6th or 7th moves: his position would not have been better developed, but White would have had to secure far more compensation. Whether the offer is sound or not cannot be determined beforehand; what can be asserted is that there is enough to make us believe that the sacrifice is worth looking into.

The rule, in other words, is a kind of Grand Jury which returns an indictment. Whether the charges will be upheld or not depends upon the course of the game.

In No. 19 (Nimzovitch-Capablanca, St. Petersburg, 1914) we see the results of a sacrifice to deflect White's Queen. Time must now be lost to bring the Queen back into play; meanwhile Black will be fully developed and will build up counterplay. The opening moves were: 1 P—K4, P—K4; 2 Kt—KB3, Kt—QB3; 3 B—Kt5, P—Q3; 4 P—Q4,

B—Q2; 5 Kt—B3, Kt—B3; 6 B×Kt, B×B; 7 Q—Q3, P×P; 8 Kt×P, P—KKt3; 9 Kt×B, P×Kt; 10 Q—R6, Q—Q2; 11 Q—Kt7, R—B1; 12 Q×RP, B—Kt2.

No. 19

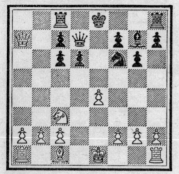

Black has given up a Pawn to deflect the White Queen.

Castling is most often prevented by placing a Bishop at QR3 covering an open diagonal. No. 20 is typical. It comes from the following variation of the Evans Gambit; 1 P—K4, P—K4; 2 Kt—KB3, Kt—QB3; 3 B—B4, B—B4; 4 P—QKt4, B×P; 5 P—B3, B—R4; 6 P—Q4, P×P; 7 O—O, KKt—K2; 8 P×P, P—Q4; P×P, KKt×P; 10 B—R3, B—K3; 11 QKt—Q2, B×Kt; 12 Q×B. To castle on the Queen's side would be highly dangerous for Black because White has two powerful open files for his Rooks. But to castle on the other side he must first block the diagonal of White's Bishop at R3, and this can only be done at the expense of a Pawn. E.g., 12 .... Kt(B3)—K2; 13 KR—K1. If now 13 .... O—O?; 14 B(B4)×Kt! wins the exchange, for on either 14 .... B×B or 14 .... Q×B the Kt is in take, while 14 .... Kt×B is answered by 15 B×R. After 13 KR—K1, P—QB3 is best, when 14 Kt—Kt5, O—O; 15 Kt×B, P×Kt; 16 R×P regains the Pawn with the better position for White.

A second method of preventing castling is that of pinning a piece on an open center file in such a way that the King is tied down to its defense. An example is No. 21 where both Queen and Rook bear down

No. 20

White has sacrificed a Pawn to prevent Black from castling.

on the Bishop. (From the Giuoco Piano. Opening moves: 1 P—K4, P—K4; 2 Kt—KB3, Kt—QB3; 3 B—B4, B—B4; 4 P—B3, Kt—B3; 5 P—Q4, P×P; 6 O—O, Kt×P?; 7 P×P, B—K2; 8 P—Q5, Kt—Kt1; 9 R—K1, Kt—KB3; 10 Q—K2.) A word of caution is necessary for such positions: with the Queen at Q1 Black may not castle, but if it is at Q2 and the White Rook is not defended he may. This becomes clear by comparing Nos. 21 and 22. In No. 21, after 1 .... O—O? 2 Q×B, R—K1; 3 Q×Q the Black Rook is pinned and can do nothing but recapture. But in No. 22 after 1 .... O—O!; 2 Q×B?, R—K1; 3 Q×Q the Rook is not pinned, Black can reply 3 .... R×Rch; 4 K—R2 and 5 .... QKt×Q and now he is the exchange and a Pawn ahead.

No. 21

White has sacrificed a Pawn to prevent Black from castling.

No. 22

Black can castle without losing his Bishop.

There is still a third method of preventing castling: compelling the King to move. No. 23 is a typical case of the effects of trying to hold on to a Pawn at the expense of King safety. (From the Staunton Gambit. Opening moves: 1 P—Q4, P—KB4; 2 P—K4, P×P; 3 Kt—QB3, Kt—KB3; 4 B—KKt5, P—KKt3; 5 P—KR4, P—Q3; 6 P—R5, B—Kt5; 7 B—K2, P×P; 8 B×Kt, P×B; 9 B×B, P×B; 10 Q×P, Q—Q2; 11 Q—R5ch, K—Q1; 12 O—O—O, P—KB4.) White should continue with 13 Kt—R3 followed by a crushing attack against the Black King position.

No. 23

In order to retain his extra Pawn Black has moved his King, thus eliminating the possibility of castling.

In all of the above cases White invariably developed a strong attack, but this was the consequence of one of the other advantages (e.g., prevention of castling) rather than the original reason for the sacrifice. An example of a sacrifice for nothing but an attack is seen in No. 24 (Mieses-Rubinstein, Breslau, 1912). Opening moves: 1 P—K4, P—K4; 2 B—B4, Kt—KB3; 3 P—Q4, P×P; 4 Kt—KB3, Kt×P; 5 Q×P, Kt—KB3; 6 B—KKt5, B—K2; 7 Kt—B3, Kt—B3; 8 Q—R4, P—Q3; 9 O—O—O, B—K3; 10 B—Q3, Q—Q2; 11 B—Kt5, O—O; 12 Kt—

Q4. There is nothing wrong with Black's development here (except that his pieces are a bit congested), yet the attacking possibilities give sufficient compensation for the Pawn.

All of these reasons can be boiled down to one subsidiary rule: Do not sacrifice a Pawn unless by so doing you disrupt the normal course of the opponent's game without hurting your own.

One essential point which must not be dismissed lightly is the question of what happens if the rules are broken. There is a strong tendency to believe that any infringement, no matter how slight, is bound to result in immediate loss. This is only so in special cases—e.g., the person who refuses to develop his pieces is bound to be overwhelmed in a short time, as is the person who gives up one piece after another "just for the fun of it." Usually if you stick to sound principles and your opponent does not you will secure an advantage. The exploitation of this advantage, the technique of winning the game when you have the better position, is a story in itself and will be treated in Chapters VI–IX.

No. 24

White has sacrificed a Pawn for a direct attack on Black's King position.

To apply the rules properly, you should remember that there are three basic elements in opening play: development, the center and time. While these three are distinct, in the actual conduct of the game they are blended into one unified force, i.e., every move must contribute something to each.

Expressed even more succinctly, the basic idea in the openings is simply this: Develop quickly and get control of the center.

This gives us two crucial questions which must be answered for every move played:

1. How does this move affect the center?
2. How does it fit in with the development of my other pieces and Pawns?

PROBLEMS

No. 7

White has just played 2 B—Kt5. Is this good or bad and why?

No. 8

Black to play. What is his best move?

No. 9

Black has just played 1 .... P—QR3. What rule or rules has he violated?

No. 10

Who has the better center position?

No. 11

Black to play. Who has the better game and why?

No. 12

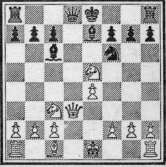

Black has given up a Pawn for this position. Is the sacrifice worth while?

Chapter V

THE OPENING

PART II

THE BASIC VARIATIONS AND IDEAS

There is more literature on chess than on all other games together. Ever since the middle of the past century, the world has been deluged with books, magazines, pamphlets, brochures, columns and occasional articles on the game. A considerable portion of this immense production has been devoted to the openings. Literally millions of variations have been discovered, analyzed, sifted, played, discarded, rejuvenated. Every day dozens of new lines appear in print. The field has become so immense that even a master is at best acquainted with only a small portion of it.

The beginner who confronts it is often bewildered. He has neither the time nor the inclination to memorize thousands of opening moves. Yet he finds that in a contest with an opponent who does "know the books" he is invariably worsted. Fortunately, however, pure rote memorization is neither necessary nor desirable. Knowledge of a few fundamental ideas and still fewer variations is sufficient.

In the previous chapter we presented a series of rules which are applicable to every opening. Now we shall explain the peculiarities and special problems which turn up in the most common ones which should be used. In this way the reader will have a concise and adequate guide to a maze which so often seems hopelessly confusing.

We strongly advise the reader to get a working knowledge of a few openings and stick to them. A rolling chess stone gathers no points. This chapter has been written with the purpose of providing such direct and highly useful knowledge. With White only the KP opening should be played. Although there is no difference in value between 1 P—K4 and 1 P—Q4 and the choice among masters is largely a matter of taste, the basic ideas in the King's Pawn openings are easier to grasp and more readily applicable, while the stock of variations required is much smaller.

Against the 1 . . . . P—K4 reply both the Ruy Lopez and the Giuoco Piano should be used. Against other defenses the lines given here as best should be played. With Black only the 1 . . . . P—K4 defense should be adopted on 1 P—K4. On 1 P—Q4 the Slav Defense is best as a starter, but should be varied with the Nimzoindian or Queen's Indian as the player improves.

First a brief review of the theoretical outlines of the opening struggle. White has a slight advantage; hence he should expect to go into the middle game with somewhat the better of it. *White's problem is to preserve his initial superiority.* Black, on the other hand, should be satisfied if he can nullify White's plus. Thus *Black's problem is to secure equality.* White *attacks*, but Black *defends.* And, of course, if both sides play perfectly (if it ever happens you'll get your money back) the game will be drawn.

1 P—K4 and 1 P—Q4 are the two strongest opening moves, because they are the only ones which promise White the advantage which is his due. While other moves are playable and often seen they require a good deal of theoretical knowledge. Since they lead to nothing lasting they cannot be recommended for the inexpert.

I. KING PAWN OPENINGS

With the opening move 1 P—K4 White aims to build up a strong Pawn center—he is going to play P—Q4 at the earliest suitable moment. Black cannot prevent P—Q4; nor can he ignore it. The best he can do is to take the sting out of it.

This gives us another test of the value of any Black defensive set-up —what it does about the threatened establishment of both White Pawns in the center.

The safest defense is the symmetrical one, *1 . . . . P—K4,* which leads to a fairly quick development on both sides and may accordingly be called the *Open Game* (See No. 25).

The central idea back of this defense is to preserve a Pawn at K4. This does not mean that the Pawn at K4 will never under any circumstances be removed. Play White's Queen to Q4 and the Black Pawn will grab with alacrity. It does

No. 25. The Open Game.

Black's central strategical idea is to preserve a Pawn at K4.

mean that the KP will not be exchanged unless *adequate compensation* for the dissolution of this Rock of Gibraltar is secured. This compensation *must* involve the removal or weakening of the enemy KP.

E.g., if White plays 2 P—Q4 (known as the Center Game), the reply 2 .... P—Q3 would transpose into inferior lines in other openings, but 2 .... P×P!; 3 Q×P, Kt—QB3; 4 Q—K3, Kt—KB3; gives Black an excellent position because he is ahead in development and will soon rid himself of the White KP. If White does not choose to play a gambit, the following continuation is then forced: 5 Kt—QB3, B—Kt5; 6 B—Q2, O—O; 7 O—O—O, R—K1; 8 P—B3, P—Q4; 9 Q—B2, P×P; 10 Kt×P, B×Bch; 11 R×B, Q—K2; 12 Kt×Ktch, Q×Kt; 13 B—B4, Kt—K4; 14 B—Kt3, P—QR4. Black has a free game, his pieces are aggressively placed, he has a good attack. Thus we say that Black stands better. Such an opening cannot be good for the first player.

Against any anti-theoretical move on White's part Black can get at least an even game by an early counter in the center. E.g., if 2 P—KKt3?, Kt—KB3; 3 B—Kt2, P—Q4 and Black stands well. Or, to take a stronger line: 2 B—B4 (Bishop's Opening), 2 .... Kt—KB3; 3 P—Q3, P—B3! (preparing .... P—Q4); 4 P—B4, P×P; 5 B×P, P—Q4; 6 P×P, Kt×P and Black already has equality. Hence White must not only try to get in P—Q4 himself, but must also try to block the symmetrical move by his opponent. Fortunately, normal aggressive developing moves make a counter-attack by Black extremely risky and often lead to immediate loss.

Except for gambit lines (which will be treated separately) the only continuation consonant with correct opening principles is *2 Kt—KB3*. While this does not threaten to win the KP at once (e.g., 2 .... P—QR3?; 3 Kt×P, Q—K2; 4 P—Q4, P—Q3; 5 Kt—KB3, Q×Pch and Black has regained his Pawn) it will soon do so. If e.g., 2 .... P—QR3?; 3 Kt—QB3 the Pawn can no longer be offered.

Of the various direct methods of defending the KP, only one is really good: *2 .... Kt—QB3*. The alternative 2 .... P—KB3 (Damiano's Defence) weakens the King position and is refuted by 3 Kt×P!, Q—K2; 4 Kt—KB3, Q×Pch; 5 B—K2 and White besides being appreciably ahead in development will gain further time by harassing the exposed Black Queen. 2 .... Q—K2, or 2 .... Q—B3 violate our sixth rule.

2 .... B—Q3 is inferior because it blocks the development of the other Black pieces (see discussion of fourth rule). 2 .... P—Q3 is playable, but leads to a cramped position. 2 .... P—Q3; 3 P—Q4, Kt—Q2; 4 B—QB4, P—QB3; 5 P—QR4, B—K2; 6 Kt—B3, KKt—B3; 7 O—O, O—O; 8 P—QKt3, Q—B2; 9 B—R3 and Black has many problems. Such openings are particularly dangerous because any further inferior move is apt to be fatal.

Thus here after 1 P—K4, P—K4; 2 Kt—KB3, P—Q3; 3 P—Q4, B—Kt5? is an error frequently seen.   4 P×P, B×Kt; 5 Q×B, P×P; 6 B—QB4, Kt—KB3; 7 Q—QKt3 then wins a Pawn, for both the KBP and the QKtP are en prise.

Instead of defending his KP, Black sometimes goes in for a counter-attack against the enemy KP.   One such attack is 2 .... P—KB4 (Greco Counter Gambit).   This is best met by 3 Kt×P, Q—B3; 4 P—Q4, P—Q3; 5 Kt—B4, P×P; 6 Kt—B3, Q—Kt3; 7 B—B4, Kt—KB3; 8 Kt—K3, B—K2; 9 B—B4, P—B3; 10 P—Q5! (Black must be prevented from consolidating his center), P—Kt4; 11 B—K2 and White has much the better of it: he is ahead in development and his pieces are more effectively placed.   A more subdued line is 2 .... Kt—KB3 (Petroff's Defense).   Against this 3 Kt×P, P—Q3; 4 Kt—KB3, Kt×P; 5 P—Q4, P—Q4; 6 B—Q3, B—Q3; 7 O—O, O—O; 8 P—B4, P—QB3; 9 Kt—B3 leaves White slightly ahead in development.   Incidentally, there is a cute trap in the "You take mine, I'll take yours" variation here: 1 P—K4, P—K4; 2 Kt—KB3, Kt—KB3; 3 Kt×P, Kt×P?; 4 Q—K2!, Kt—KB3; 5 Kt—B6 dis ch and the Black monarch will soon be a widower.

Let us return to the chief line: 1 P—K4, P—K4; 2 Kt—KB3, Kt—QB3.   White then has the choice of four different continuations:

A. 3 P—Q4 (Scotch Game), played with a view to establishing a strong piece in the center.

B. 3 B—B4 (Giuoco Piano and Two Knights' Defense), preventing .... P—Q4 by Black and preparing P—QB3 followed by P—Q4.   If successful, White will have an ideal Pawn center.

C. 3 B—Kt5 (Ruy Lopez), to exert continuous pressure on the Black KP and center.

D. 3 Kt—B3 (Four Knights' Game), hoping that the extra move in a symmetrical position may lead to something.

Of these B and C are most important, for they are the hardest to meet.

A. SCOTCH GAME (3 P—Q4)

The strength of this advance lies in the fact that Black is practically compelled to exchange his KP.   For if 3 .... P—Q3 the reply 4 P×P, P×P; 5 Q×Qch, K×Q; 6 Kt—B3, P—B3; 7 B—K3, B—K3; 8 O—O—Och gives White an appreciable advantage in development. After 3 .... P—Q3; 4 B—Kt5 likewise transposes into a favorable variation of the Ruy Lopez.

But the weakness of the Scotch Game is that Black can liquidate the enemy KP too quickly by countering with .... P—Q4 at the appropriate time.   Thus the main equalizing line is, beginning from

No. 26, 3 .... P×P; 4 Kt×P, Kt—B3; 5 Kt—QB3, B—Kt5; 6 Kt×
Kt, KtP×Kt; 7 B—Q3, P—Q4; 8 P×P, P×P; 9 O—O, O—O;
10 B—KKt5, B—K3 and Black has nothing to fear.

B. GIUOCO PIANO AND TWO KNIGHTS' DEFENSE (3 B—B4)

In the Giuoco Piano (Italian for "Quiet Game") White develops his
Bishop at B4 in order to prevent the Black counter-thrust in the center.

No. 26

Scotch Game.

While Black can play this advance
only at the cost of a Pawn, in some
cases the sacrifice is worth while.

The Giuoco Piano proper occurs
after 3 .... B—B4; 4 P—B3 (see
No. 27). Against passive or inferior
play the execution of the White
plan will net him a powerful center
and a freer development. E.g.,
4 .... P—Q3?; 5 P—Q4, P×P; 6
P×P, B—Kt3; 7 Kt—B3; Kt—B3;
8 Q—Q3 (to avoid the pin of the
KKt by .... B—KKt5), B—Kt5;
9 B—K3, O—O; 10 P—QR3, R—
K1; 11 B—R2 (note A.) Q—Q2;
12 Kt—Q2, R—K2; 13 O—O, QR
—K1; 14 P—B3, B—KR4 and

White has a clear advantage (see No. 28). He has two strong center
Pawns and his pieces control more space. Note A. The threat was
11 .... Kt×KP; 12 Kt×Kt, P—Q4, ruining White's center.

To prevent the formation of such a powerful Pawn center with its

No. 27

Giuoco Piano.

No. 28

Ideal position for White in the Giuoco
Piano. White has an advantage.

cramping effect on Black's game, the second player can choose one of
two defenses: he can either play for an immediate counter-attack, or
he can maintain a Pawn in the center. The first is tactical and full of
traps which tempt the unwary; the second is solid but less spectacular.

A counter-attack by Black, if it is to have any meaning, must affect
the center directly. Thus: 4 .... Kt—B3, threatening the KP and
preparing .... P—Q4. If now 5 P—Q3?, P—Q4 equalizes. Best play
after 4 .... Kt—B3 runs as follows:

5 P—Q4, P×P; 6 P×P, B—Kt5ch; 7 Kt—B3, Kt×KP (Note A);
8 O—O, B×Kt (Note B); 9 P—Q5, Kt—K4; 10 P×B, Kt×B; 11 Q—
Q4!, P—KB4! (Note C); 12 Q×Kt(B4), P—Q3; 13 Kt—Q4, O—O;
14 R—Kt1, P—QKt3 and White has just about enough compensation
for his Pawn.

To understand this variation better a number of branch lines must
be explored.

Note A. If White does not wish to sacrifice a Pawn, he must play
7 B—Q2, when 7 .... B×Bch; 8 QKt×B, P—Q4!; 9 P×P, KKt×P
gives Black immediate equality. All his pieces are well developed, he
occupies an important central post, White's Queen's Pawn may eventually become weak.

Note B. If Black on move 8 exchanges Kt for Kt, instead of B for
Kt he can at best hope to draw with much difficulty. The trap, first
discovered almost four hundred years ago by Greco, runs as follows:
8 .... Kt×Kt; 9 P×Kt, B×P; 10 Q—Kt3 (see No. 29), B×R?;
11 B×Pch, K—B1; 12 B—Kt5, Kt—K2; 13 R—K1, P—KR3; 14 B—
Kt6! (threatening Q—B7 mate), P—Q4; 15 B×Ktch, Q×B; 16 R×Q,
K×R; 17 Q—K3ch, K—Q1; 18 Q—B1, B×P; 19 Kt×B and White
is in effect a piece ahead and will win quickly (See Chapter VI).

The only defense in the diagrammed position (No. 29) is 10
.... P—Q4; 11 B×P, O—O; 12
B×Pch, K—R1; 13 Q×B, R×B.
Black has maintained material
equality, but his position is slightly
inferior.

Note C. Black must not try to
hold on to the extra piece because
he would then expose himself to a
mating attack. We begin from No.
30. On 11 .... Kt(B5)—Q3?; 12
Q×KtP wins: 12 .... Q—B3;
13 Q×Q, Kt×Q; 14 R—K1ch, K—
B1; 15 B—R6ch, K—Kt1; 16 R—
K5, Kt(B3)—K5; 17 R—K1, P—
KB4; 18 R—K7, P—Kt3; 19 Kt—

No. 29

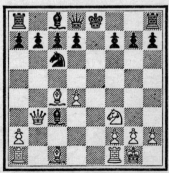

Black to play. Trap in the Giuoco Piano.
10 .... B×R? loses. 10 .... P—Q4
is necessary.

R4, B—Kt2; 20 R—Kt7ch, K—B1; 21 R×RP dis ch, K—Kt1; 22 R—Kt7ch, K—B1; 23 Kt—Kt6ch, K—K1; 24 Kt×R. White is now the exchange and a Pawn ahead and also threatens to win a piece by 25 P—B3. The conclusion should be simple.

The second type of defense at Black's disposal involves maintaining his Pawn at K4.

No. 30

Black to play. Trap in the Giuoco Piano. 11 .... Kt(B5)—Q3 loses; 11 .... P—KB4 is necessary.

The KP can be supported only by the QP, for the advance of the KBP would weaken the King position. But unfortunately if 4 .... P—Q3 at once (in No. 27) 5 P—Q4 compels Black to exchange Pawns. For on 5 P—Q4, B—Kt3? loses a Pawn: 6 P×P, P×P; 7 Q×Qch, and 7 .... Kt×Q is met by 8 Kt×P, while 7 .... K×Q is answered by 8 B×P. Consequently the point K4 must be held in some other way. The B has already moved, besides, ... B—Q3 is a violation of principle. Only the Q sortie 4 .... Q—K2 remains. Now 5 P—Q4 begins the following sequence of moves: 5 P—Q4, B—Kt3; 6 O—O, Kt—B3; 7 R—K1, P—Q3; 8 P—QR4, P—QR3; 9 P—R3 (to prevent the pin), O—O; 10 P—QKt4, P—KR3; 11 B—R3, Kt—Q2; 12 P—Kt5, Kt—Q1; 13 QKt—Q2, Q—B3. While White controls somewhat more space, Black's game is perfectly solid. This variation can only be recommended for the conservative player.

The fact that White retains somewhat more freedom for his pieces shows that the opening is good for him. On the other hand, since Black has no serious weaknesses he cannot be said to have a bad game.

To recapitulate: Black has the choice of two defenses in No. 27. In the aggressive one (4 .... Kt—B3) White usually sacrifices a Pawn for the attack, but Black can defend himself with best play. In the solid defense (4 .... Q—K2) Black's object is to keep his Pawn at K4, supporting it by .... P—Q3 at the earliest suitable moment. The drawback of this line is that the Black position remains somewhat cramped.

The Two Knights' Defense (No. 31) is an attempt to wrest the initiative from White at the cost of a Pawn. If he wishes to try to retain an advantage, White must accept the sacrifice. Thus the best line for both is 4 Kt—Kt5, P—Q4; 5 P×P, Kt—QR4 (Note A); 6 B—Kt5ch (Note B), P—B3; 7 P×P, P×P; 8 B—K2, P—KR3; 9 Kt—KB3, P—K5; 10 Kt—K5, B—Q3; 11 P—KB4, O—O; 12 O—O,

B×Kt; 13 P×B, Q—Q5ch; 14 K—
R1, Q×KP; 15 P—Q4, P×P e.p.;
16 Q×P (No. 32) and White's
game is preferable.

Note A. The immediate recapture of the Pawn is bad for Black:
5 .... Kt×P; 6 P—Q4, B—K3; 7
Kt×B, P×Kt; 8 P×P, Kt×P;
9 Q—R5ch, Kt—B2; 10 O—O, B
—Q3; 11 R—K1 and wins a Pawn.

An alternative possibility for
Black is 5 .... P—QKt4; 6 B—B1,
Kt×P; 7 B×P, B—Kt2; 8 P—
Q3, P—KR3; 9 Kt—KB3, B—Q3,
although here too White retains a
clear advantage.

Note B. 6 P—Q3 is inferior. The continuation would then be 6
.... P—KR3; 7 Kt—KB3, P—K5; 8 Q—K2, Kt×B; 9 P×Kt, B—
QB4; 10 KKt—Q2, O—O; 11 Kt—Kt3, B—KKt5; 12 Q—B1, B—
Kt5ch; 13 Kt—B3, P—QKt4, when Black has sufficient compensation
for the Pawn.

Against inferior play White should strive to set up his ideal development: both Pawns in the center, Knights at B3, B's at B4 or Kt5, all
pieces as aggressively placed as possible. Once his development is
completed it will be time to start an attack, especially if the Black
King has been weakened.

There are, however, a number of cases where an attack against the
Black King is justifiable at an earlier stage. We have already pointed
out that the Pawn at KB2 is the Achilles' heel in Black's position. If
he makes normal moves he will,
nevertheless, always be able to defend this point. But one weak move
which leaves it exposed may well
cost him the game. The typical trap
is seen in No. 33 (Black has just
played 4 .... KKt—K2? instead
of 4 .... Kt—B3). After 5 Kt—
KKt5! Black is lost: 5 .... O—O;
6 Q—R5, threatening both Q×RP
mate and Kt×KBP. Black can
only defend one point: 6 .... P—
KR3; 7 Kt×P, R×Kt; 8 Q×Rch
and wins (exchange and a Pawn
ahead).

The vulnerability of this point

No. 31

Two Knights' Defense.

No. 32

Position arrived at in Two Knights'
Defense. White's game is superior.

No. 33

White to play wins.

also leads to other traps, especially if Black develops his Bishop at KKt5 before his King side is adequately developed. E.g., 1 P—K4, P—K4; 2 Kt—KB3, Kt—QB3; 3 B—B4, P—Q3; 4 Kt—B3, P—KR3; 5 P—Q4, B—Kt5?; 6 P×P, Kt×P??; 7 Kt×Kt!, B×Q; 8 B×Pch, K—K2; 9 Kt—Q5 mate. This is known as Legal's Trap (see also No. 45).

Against inferior play on White's part Black secures an even game by an early advance of his QP. Traps similar to that in No. 33 occur, but much less frequently, since White is one move ahead.

C. RUY LOPEZ

In this opening White does not attempt to force a strong Pawn center at an early stage (as in the Giuoco Piano) but hopes that the continued pressure on Black's QKt and KP will eventually compel an exchange of the center Pawn. To counter the pressure Black again has two defenses, one holding the Pawn at K4, the other exchanging it but securing White's KP in return.

An examination of No. 34 reveals a curious situation. White obviously threatens something, but if we look closer we find that he threatens .... to threaten! E.g., if it were White's move and he played 4 B×Kt, the reply 4 .... QP×B; 5 Kt×P, Q—Q5; 6 Kt—KB3, Q×KPch regains the Pawn for Black. Yet, if White castled, the KP would then really be en prise. Consequently Black has, in a sense, an extra tempo to do anything he wishes to. We shall soon see how this tempo may be put to use.

The ideal set-up for White is shown in No. 35. His game is freer, he has a piece strongly posted in the center, and his KP is stronger than Black's QP.

To avoid this type of disadvantage, Black can do one of two things: he can hold on to his Pawn at K4 (Close Defense) or he can try to get rid of White's KP (Open Defense). Before proceeding we have to go back to the days of the flood for a minute. The story goes that to while away the dreary hours on the ark and to steel themselves against the raging waters, Noah and his sons were in the habit of playing chess. One of the games which was recorded and used as a warning for the future, ran as follows: 1 P—K4, P—K4; 2 Kt—KB3,

No. 34   No. 35

Ruy Lopez.   Ruy Lopez. Ideal position for White.

Kt—QB3; 3 B—Kt5, P—QR3; 4 B—R4, P—Q3; 5 P—Q4, P—QKt4;
6 B—Kt3, Kt×P; 7 Kt×Kt, P×Kt; 8 Q×P, P—QB4; 9 Q—Q5,
B—K3; 10 Q—B6ch, B—Q2; 11 Q—Q5, P—B5 and Black wins a
piece. This has since been known as The Noah's Ark Trap.

Now, since White is going to play P—Q4 at some future date, and
since Black wants to have an adequate defense ready, he may try to
prepare The Noah's Ark Trap. Of course, he will not expect to get it
over but, as the saying goes, the threat may be stronger than its ful-
fillment.

Since Black has an extra move
at his disposal, he might as well
play 3 .... P—QR3. This move
not only improves every available
defense, but is the only feasible
method of preventing P—Q4 at an
early stage. Why this is so will be
seen in the individual variations.

No. 36

The older defenses to the Ruy
Lopez usually began with 3 ....
Kt—KB3, or 3 .... P—Q3 and
the game would proceed as follows:
3 .... Kt—KB3; 4 O—O, P—Q3;
5 P—Q4, B—Q2; 6 Kt—B3, B—
K2; 7 R—K1 (see No. 36). Now
Black is finally compelled to give up

Ruy Lopez. Black to play must not
castle.

the center, for if 7 .... O—O? White wins a Pawn (this is known as
the Dresden Trap). 8 B×Kt, B×B; 9 P×P, P×P; 10 Q×Q, QR×Q
(or note A); 11 Kt×P, B×P; 12 Kt×B, Kt×Kt; 13 Kt—Q3, P—
KB4; 14 P—B3, B—B4ch; 15 Kt×B, Kt×Kt; 16 B—Kt5, R—Q4;
17 B—K7, R—B2; 18 P—QB4 and Black must lose the exchange.

A. If 10 .... KR×Q; 11 Kt×P, B×P; 12 Kt×B, Kt×Kt; 13 Kt—Q3, P—KB4; 14 P—B3, B—B4ch; 15 K—B1, and wins a piece.

Consequently 7 .... P×P; 8 Kt×P is forced. If now 8 .... O—O; 9 B—B1 White has the ideal position. Best is 8 .... Kt×Kt (in a cramped position one should exchange as many pieces as possible); 9 Q×Kt, B×B; 10 Kt×B, O—O; 11 P—QB4 but White maintains an advantage.

Now suppose that we insert the moves .... P—QR3, B—R4 in

No. 37

Ruy Lopez Close Defense. The chances are about even. White will attack on the King's side, Black on the other wing.

No. 36. Then on P—Q4 Black could reply .... P—QKt4 and if B—Kt3, P×P; Kt×P, Kt×Kt; Q×Kt, P—B4, winning a piece (old Noah again). As a result, if Black has played 3 .... P—QR3, this variation will no longer be feasible for White. This leaves him only the alternative of preparing P—Q4 by P—B3, but this is slow and adequate counter-steps can be taken. These steps consist of keeping the QP under constant attack by playing .... P—QB4.

The best line in the Close Defense runs as follows: (1 P—K4, P—K4; 2 Kt—KB3, Kt—QB3; 3 B—Kt5), P—QR3; 4 B—R4, Kt—B3; 5 O—O (note A), B—K2; 6 R—K1 (note B), P—QKt4 (note C); 7 B—Kt3, P—Q3; 8 P—B3, Kt—QR4; 9 B—B2, P—B4; 10 P—Q4, Q—B2; 11 P—KR3, Kt—B3; 12 P—Q5, Kt—Q1; 13 QKt—Q2, O—O; 14 Kt—B1, P—B5 with about even chances. (No. 37). This line, however, requires considerable ability in judging defense possibilities and, while it is perfectly correct, should not be attempted by the less experienced.

Note A. If 5 P—Q4, P×P gives Black at least an even game, for 6 Kt×P?, Kt×Kt; 7 Q×Kt, P—QKt4; 8 B—Kt3, P—B4; 9 Q—K5ch, B—K2, while not quite as bad as Noah's Trap, still leaves Black ahead in development.

Note B. 6 P—Q4, P×P now involves the old danger of Noah's Ark.

Note C. Black must not play too passively. White is threatening to win a Pawn by 7 B×Kt and 8 Kt×P. If 6 .... P—Q3; 7 P—B3, O—O; 8 P—Q4 again threatens a Pawn capture and Black will have no time to get his QKt out of the way and advance .... P—B4.

Against inferior play by Black White will secure a strong Pawn center which will cramp Black's game (continued pressure on the Kt at B6 will compel the exchange of Black's KP for White's QP). Incorrect play by White should be punished, as usual, by an early advance of the Black QP or capture of the White KP. E.g., in the main variation, if, instead of 6 R—K1, 6 P—Q3, O—O; 7 P—B3?, P—QKt4; 8 B—B2, P—Q4 Black already has at least equality. Whenever the capture of the KP is possible without exposing the Kt to an eventual pin after White moves P —Q4, it should be played. E.g., after 5 .... B—K2, if 6 P—B3 (instead of 6 R—K1), Kt×P equalizes at once, for now 7 P—Q4, P×P is meaningless for White, while 7 R— K1 is met by 7 .... Kt—B4.

No. 38

Ruy Lopez Open Defense. The chances are about even.

In the Open Defense Black takes a different tack. Instead of trying to hold on to his own KP, he will get rid of White's, thus securing a free and easy development for his pieces. This line runs as follows: (1 P—K4, P—K4; 2 Kt—KB3, Kt—QB3; 3 B—Kt5), P—QR3; 4 B—R4, Kt—B3; 5 O—O, Kt×P; 6 P—Q4, P—QKt4 (note A); 7 B—Kt3, P—Q4; 8 P×P, B—K3; 9 P—B3 (note B), B—K2; 10 Q—K2, O—O; 11 QKt—Q2, Kt—B4; 12 Kt—Q4, Kt×B!; 13 Kt(Q2)×Kt (note C), Q—Q2; 14 Kt×Kt, Q×Kt; (No. 38) and again the position is about even.

Note A. Black must not expose his Kt to the pin on the open K file. If 6 .... P×P?; 7 R—K1, P—Q4; 8 Kt×P (threatening P—B3) the best that Black can do is choose the Riga Variation: 8 ...., B—Q3; 9 Kt×Kt, B×Pch; 10 K—R1!, Q—R5; 11 R×Ktch!, P×R; 12 Q—Q8ch!, Q×Q; 13 Kt×Qdis ch, K×Kt; 14 K×B, and White will win the ending.

Note B. White must preserve his valuable Bishop for the time being.

Note C. A pretty combination: if 13 Kt(Q4)×Kt(B6), Kt×B!; 14 Kt×Q??, Kt×Qch and wins (15 K—R1, QR×Kt and Black is two pieces ahead).

Against inferior play on Black's part in this variation White can advance his KBP and secure a powerful attack. E.g., in the main line, leading to No. 38, if 10 B—K3, O—O; 11 QKt—Q2, Kt×Kt!; 12 Q×Kt, Kt—R4 is essential. But if 10 B—K3, Kt—R4?; 11 Kt—Q4, O—O; 12 P—B3, Kt—B4; 13 B—QB2, Kt—B5; 14 B—B1, Kt×KP; 15 P—QKt4, Kt—Kt2; 16 P—KB4, Kt—B5; 17 Q—Q3, P—Kt3;

18 P—B5!, B—Q2; 19 B—R6, R—K1; 20 P×P, RP×P; 21 R×P!, K×R; 22 Q×P mate.

Against inferior play on White's part Black should move his Q-side majority up and secure strong counterplay in the center (.... P—QB4 and .... P—Q5 at the right time). In addition, if White plays passively, his KP may become very weak.

D. FOUR KNIGHTS' GAME

In this opening White relies solely on his extra move. The development is as a rule symmetrical and there are few traps involved. The main consideration for both sides is time—the pieces must be brought into play without delay of any kind. Unnecessary Pawn moves (such as P—KR3 to prevent a pin) must be shunned as the plague.

No. 39

Four Knights' Game.

The Four Knights' proper (sometimes called the Spanish, or Ruy Lopez Four Knights') is seen in No. 39. Against a passive move such as 4 .... B—K2, the reply 5 O—O threatens B×Kt and Kt×KP. Consequently 5 .... P—Q3 is forced, when 6 P—Q4 transposes into a favorable variation of the Ruy Lopez (No. 36). So Black must develop his Bishop somewhere else.

On 4 .... B—B4; 5 Kt×P! gets rid of Black's KP (see Rule 9, discussion). E.g., 5 Kt×P, Kt ×Kt; 6 P—Q4, B—Kt5; 7 P×Kt, Kt×P; 8 Q—Kt4 and White should win. Thus there remains only 4 .... B—Kt5, which compels Black to continue symmetrically. Best play is then 5 O—O, O—O; 6 P—Q3, P—Q3; 7 Kt—K2 (Note A), Kt—K2; 8 P—B3, B—R4; 9 Kt—Kt3, P—B3; 10 B—R4, Kt— Kt3; 11 P—Q4, P—Q4! with equality (No. 40). In this final position, if 12 P×QP, P—K5; 13 Kt—K5, P×P is good for Black, while 12 P×KP, Kt(B3)×P; 13 Kt×Kt, P×Kt; 14 Kt—Kt5, Kt×P; 15 Kt×P liquidates all the center Pawns, which solves Black's opening problem.

Note A. In the other symmetrical variation, beginning with 7 B— Kt5, Black must break by 7 .... B×Kt; 8 P×B, Q—K2, when he likewise has a good game. But if on 7 B—Kt5, B—Kt5?; 8 Kt—Q5, Kt—Q5; 9 B—QB4, B—QB4; 10 Q—Q2!, P—B3; 11 Kt×Ktch, P×Kt; 12 B—R4, B×Kt; 13 Q—R6, Kt—K7ch; 14 K—R1, B×Pch;

15 K×B, Kt—B5ch; 16 K—R1, Kt—Kt3; 17 P—Q4, B×P; 18 P—QB3, B—Kt3; 19 QR—Q1, Q—K2; 20 R—KKt1, K—R1; 21 R—Q3, R—KKt1; 22 R—R3, R—Kt2; 23 R—B3 and wins by 24 QB×P.

Against weak play on Black's part in this variation White will be able to set up a strong Pawn center. E.g., in No. 40, 11 .... R—K1 (instead of 11 .... P—Q4); 12 B —Kt3!, P×P; 13 P×P, B—K3; 14 Kt—Kt5, B×B; 15 Q×B and White stands better. As usual, an anti-theoretical move by White must be met by an early advance in the center.

No. 40

Four Knights' Game. The position is even.

The Rubinstein Defense is a popular answer to the Four Knights', but requires a good deal of theoretical knowledge. It is 4 .... Kt—Q5 in No. 39. Now 5 B—R4, B—B4!; 6 Kt×P wins a Pawn for White, but on 6 .... O—O he must submit to a dangerous attack. This variation can only be played if one is familiar with the published analysis.

If White plays his Bishop to QB4 instead of Kt5, we have the Italian or Giuoco Piano Four Knights'. However, the order of moves must be inverted: 1 P—K4, P—K4; 2 Kt—KB3, Kt—QB3; 3 B—B4, B—B4; 4 Kt—B3, Kt—B3; and *not* 3 Kt—B3, Kt—B3; 4 B—B4?, for then Black secures an easily even game by 4 .... Kt×P!. E.g., 5 B×Pch, K×B; 6 Kt×Kt, P—Q4 and Black has the better of it, or

No. 41

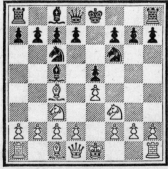

Four Knights' Game. Giuoco Piano Variation.

5 Kt×Kt, P—Q4; 6 B—Q3, P×Kt; 7 B×P, B—Q3; 8 P—Q4, P×P; 9 Kt×P, Kt×Kt with equality.

When both sides have all Knights and the two King Bishops out, we have No. 41. Normal development for both sides would now go as follows: 5 O—O note (A), O—O; 6 P—Q3, P—Q3 (note B); 7 B—KKt5 (note C), P—KR3; 8 B—R4 (No. 42), B—K3! (note D). This position is again about even.

Note A. To secure R+P for B +Kt would be a mistake here because the Black minor pieces are too actively placed. Thus: 5 Kt—

KKt5?, O—O; 6 Kt×BP, R×Kt; 7 B×Rch, K×B; 8 O—O, P—Q4; and Black stands better.

Note B. It is always bad in this opening to try to prevent the pin by the enemy Queen Bishop. The reason is that the move of the RP costs time and thereby permits an advance in the center. E.g., 6 .... P—KR3?; 7 B—K3, P—Q3; 8 P—Q4, P×P; 9 Kt×P, Kt×Kt; 10 B×Kt, B×B; 11 Q×B, R—K1; 12 QR—Q1 and White's pieces occupy more space, while he retains the theoretical advantage of a strong Pawn at K4 vs. a weak one at Q3.

No. 42

Giuoco Piano Four Knights'. Black to play. 8 .... P—KKt4? is a mistake; 8 .... B—K3 is the only correct move.

Note C. If, instead of 7 B—KKt5, White plays 7 B—K3, he is threatening to secure an advantage in the center by the thrust P—Q4. This is most effectively countered by 7 .... B—K3; for if then 8 KB×B, P×B; 9 P—Q4, P×P; 10 Kt×P, B×Kt; 11 B×B, Kt×B; 12 Q×Kt, P—K4 it is Black who has the stronger center Pawns.

Diagram No. 42 illustrates the type of position where it is fatal to weaken the Pawns near the King. If 8 .... P—KKt4?; 9 Kt×KtP!, P×Kt; 10 B×P, B—K3; 11 K—R1, K—Kt2 (to release the pin); 12 P—B4, Q—Q2; 13 P×P, Kt—KKt5; 14 B—B6ch, K—Kt1; 15 Q—B3, Kt—Q5; 16 Q—Kt3, P×P; 17 P—R3, B×B; 18 P×B, Kt—K3; 19 Q×Ktch, K—R2; 20 Q—R5ch, K—Kt1; 21 Q—R8 mate. While this mate is not forced, it can only be avoided at the expense of heavy sacrifice in material.

Note D. Again, Black must not make some non-committal move which would allow the disruption of the Pawn position defending the King. E.g., 8 .... Kt—QR4?; 9 Kt—Q5, Kt×B; 10 P×Kt, B—KKt5; 11 Q—Q2!, B×Kt; 12 Kt×Ktch, P×Kt; 13 Q×P and Black must give up his Queen to stop mate after 13 .... B×KP; 14 B×P.

On 8 .... B—K3; 9 Kt—Q5 leads to nothing because Black can capture the Kt: 9 .... B×Kt; 10 P×B, Kt—Q5; 11 Kt×Kt, B×Kt; 12 P—B3, B—Kt3 and Black stands well.

To break in the center with P—Q4, and to avert the ruining of the Pawn position near the King are the two central ideas for both sides. Weak moves should be utilized in one of these two ways. The second possibility is more serious and should be exploited by a smashing attack.

THE GAMBITS

The foregoing discussion is largely positional in character and supplies the strategical bases for the beginning of the game. There are, however, openings where one player (usually White) refuses to stick to conventional rules and sacrifices one or more Pawns for the attack. These openings are known as *gambits*. When the sacrifices are accepted and the defender tries to hold on to the material won at all costs, he finds that the attacks and combinations involved are so intricate that one who is unfamiliar with them will almost inevitably go astray. Yet even correct defense by a master leads to positions where the Pawn or Pawns ahead are of doubtful value. Consequently the best defensive tactics for practical purposes are (figuratively!) to stick your tongue out at the opponent: *take the material sacrificed, accept the gambit, but concentrate on speedy and sound development, if necessary returning the extra material in order to secure a free and easy position.*

All the gambits are based on the extreme vulnerability of Black's KB2. It is therefore imperative for the defender to see to it that this point is never neglected. In particular, the possibility of one of several typical combinations which will be pointed out should be taken into consideration.

The three chief gambits after 1 P—K4, P—K4 are 2 P—KB4 (King's), 2 P—Q4, P×P; 3 P—QB3, (Danish), and 2 Kt—KB3, Kt—QB3; 3 B—B4, B—B4; 4 P—QKt4 (Evans).

E. KING'S GAMBIT

This occurs after 1 P—K4, P—K4; 2 P—KB4 (No. 43). The best defense is 2 .... P×P!; 3 Kt—KB3, Kt—KB3 (Note A); 4 Kt—B3, P—Q4!; 5 P×P (note B), Kt×P; 6 Kt×Kt, Q×Kt; 7 P—Q4, B—K2!; 8 B—Q3, P—KKt4!; 9 Q—K2, B—KB4; 10 B×B, Q×B; 11 P—KKt4, Q—Q2! (No. 44) and Black should win.

Note A. The defense 3 .... P—KKt4, while it retains the Pawn, leads to cramped and difficult positions after 4 B—B4 or 4 P—KR4.

Note B. If 5 P—K5, Kt—KR4; 6 P—Q4, P—KKt3 with an easy defense because the diagonal KKt1—QR7 has been blocked, thus obviating the possibility of an attack against Black's KB2.

The Bishop's Gambit (3 B—B4) is a little better for White. Here it is advisable to give back the Pawn in the interests of quick development: 3 B—B4, P—Q4; 4 B×P, Kt—KB3; 5 Kt—QB3, B—Kt5; 6 Kt—B3, B×Kt; 7 QP×B, P—B3; 8 B—B4, Q×Qch; 9 K×Q, O—O; 10 QB×P, Kt×P with about an even game.

The type of attack which Black must submit to if he wishes to hold on to the sacrificed material come what may is illustrated in a brilliant little game of Morphy's:[1] 1 P—K4, P—K4; 2 P—KB4, P×P; 3 Kt—KB3, P—KKt4; 4 B—B4, B—Kt2; 5 P—KR4, P—Kt5?; 6 Kt—Kt5, Kt—KR3 (the defense of KB2 forces Black to develop artificially); 7 P—Q4, P—KB3; 8 B×P!, P×Kt; 9 B×KtP, B—B3; 10 Q—Q2!, B×B; 11 P×B, Kt—B2; 12 B×Ktch, K×B; 13 Q—B4ch, K—Kt1; 14 O—O, Q—K2; 15 Kt—B3, P—B3; 16 QR—K1, P—Q3; 17 Kt—Q5!, P×Kt; 18 P×P and wins, since Black can only stave off mate for a few moves. E.g., 18 .... B—K3; 19 R×B, Q—Kt2; 20 R—K8ch, Q—B1; 21 Q×Q mate, or 21 Q—B7! mate.

No. 43

King's Gambit.

If Black declines the gambit he must develop his KB, for else White will secure a positional advantage by exchanging Black's KP for his QP. Thus: 1 P—K4, P—K4; 2 P—KB4, P—Q3?; 3 Kt—KB3, Kt—KB3; 4 Kt—B3, Kt—B3; 5 P—Q4, P×P; 6 Kt×P, B—K2; 7 B—B4, O—O; 8 Kt(Q4)—K2 and White's game is preferable.

A typical trap to be avoided occurs after the premature development of Black's QB: 1 P—K4, P—K4; 2 P—KB4, P—Q3; 3 Kt—KB3, B—Kt5?; 4 B—B4, Kt—KB3?; 5 P×P!, P×P (see No. 45); 6 B×Pch!!, K×B; 7 Kt×Pch, K—Kt1; 8 Kt×B, Kt×P; 9 Q—K2 with a fairly easy win.

No. 44

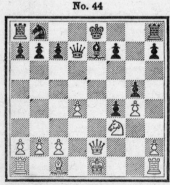

Position reached in the King's Gambit.
Black wins.

No. 45

White to play wins.

[1] Paul Morphy, 1836–1884, one of the greatest chess geniuses of all time.

The best way to decline the gambit is 2 .... B—B4! (after 1 P—K4, P—K4; 2 P—KB4), when 3 Kt—KB3, P—Q3; 4 Kt—B3, Kt—KB3; 5 B—B4, Kt—B3; 6 P—Q3, B—K3!; 7 B—Kt5, P—QR3; 8 B×Ktch, P×B; 9 Q—K2, P×P; 10 B×P, Q—Kt1!; 11 Kt—Q1, O—O; 12 P—B3, R—K1 gives about an even position, although White retains a strong initiative.

F. DANISH GAMBIT

The Danish Gambit is best countered by accepting the sacrifice and then speedily returning the extra Pawns. Thus: 1 P—K4, P—K4; 2 P—Q4, P×P; 3 P—QB3, P×P; 4 B—QB4 (note A), P×P!; 5 B×P, P—Q4!; 6 B×QP (note B), Kt—KB3!; 7 B×Pch, K×B; 8 Q×Q, B—Kt5ch; 9 Q—Q2, B×Qch; 10 Kt ×B, P—B4 with a vastly superior endgame. (No. 46). In games between masters Black almost invariably wins.

No. 46

Position reached in the Danish Gambit. Black wins.

Note A. 4 Kt×P, P—Q3; 5 B —QB4, Kt—KB3 gives White a weaker attack, but leaves Black's position rather cramped.

Note B. If 6 P×P, then 6 .... Kt—KB3 gives Black an easy defense because the dangerous diagonal of White's KB has been blocked. E.g., 7 Kt—KB3, B—Q3; 8 O—O, O—O; 9 Kt—B3, B —KKt5; 10 Q—Q4, QKt—Q2; 11 KR—K1, R—K1 and White has insufficient compensation for the Pawn.

G. EVANS GAMBIT

This too should be met by first taking the Pawn and then giving it back. Thus: 1 P—K4, P—K4; 2 Kt—KB3, Kt—QB3; 3 B—B4, B—B4; 4 P—QKt4, B×P; 5 P—B3, B—R4; 6 P—Q4, P—Q3!; 7 O— O (note A), B—Kt3! (see No. 47); 8 P×P (note B), P×P; 9 Q×Qch, Kt×Q; 10 Kt×P, B—K3 and Black has the superior endgame position (note C).

Note A. To avoid the defense given here, 7 Q—Kt3 is sometimes played, when the best reply is 7 .... Q—Q2!; 8 P×P!, B—Kt3! with approximate equality. If, however, 8 .... P×P?; 9 O—O, Kt—B3; 10 R—Q1, Q—K2; 11 B- -R3 and White wins.

Note B. On other moves Black's defense is easy. E.g., 8 Q—Kt3, Q—B3, or 8 B—R3, B—Kt5; 9 B—Kt5, P×P; 10 P×P, B×Kt; 11 B×Ktch, P×B; 12 Q×B, Kt—K2 and White does not have enough for the Pawn.

Note C. This is due to the fact that his Pawns are connected, while White's are separated. See also Chapter VIII.

No. 47

Lasker Defense to the Evans Gambit.

The typical attack if Black is too greedy runs as follows: 4 .... B×P; 5 P—B3, B—R4; 6 P—Q4, P×P; 7 O—O, Kt—B3; 8 B—R3!, P—Q3; 9 P—K5!, P—Q4 (note 1); 10 B—Kt5, Kt—K5; 11 P×P and Black is in a bad way because he cannot castle.

Note 1. If 9 .... P×KP?; 10 R —K1, B—KKt5; 11 Kt×KP! and wins, for if 11 .... B×Q; 12 B×P mate.

All defenses which do not begin with 1 .... P—K4 lead to a *Close Game*. The principles of rapid development and control of the center are equally important, but take different forms. As a rule these defenses are more complicated and require a greater knowledge of position play. While none can be recommended for the inexperienced player, it is well to know how to proceed against them with White.

The four most common ones will be discussed here.

H. FRENCH DEFENSE (1 P—K4, P—K3)

We saw above that almost all dangerous attacks in the open game are based on the exposed Black King's Bishop Pawn. Such attacks usually involve placing the White Bishop at QB4. It was also shown that if Black could succeed in blocking this Bishop (counter .... P— Q4) he could invariably secure an even game. This gives the underlying idea of Black in the French Defense: to block the diagonal KKt1—QR7 and thus make any direct aggressive action against the Black King impossible.

However, there are two drawbacks to this defense. One is that it does not place a Pawn in the center immediately, which gives White time to get the ideal Pawn position with KP and QP. Consequently Black in effect concedes his opponent a healthier center in the hope that he will be able to neutralize it at some later stage. The second objection is that the diagonal of Black's QB is blocked so that this piece remains a problem for some time.

The Pawn structure dictates the strategical outlines of the game. Black will do everything in his power to remove or weaken the strong White Pawn center and to secure some freedom for his Bishop. White will try to maintain his hold on the center and at the same time keep Black's pieces cramped.

After the opening moves the best continuation is 2 P—Q4, P—Q4. In order to free his game Black will have to attack the White center by .... P—QB4. It is a serious positional blunder for Black to block the QBP with his QKt, for he thereby gives up all hope of ever neutralizing White's powerful QP. But, as in similar cases in the open game, the break .... P—QB4 must be postponed until a suitable moment if White continues properly.

No. 48

Position reached in the French Defense. White stands better.

Thus 3 Kt—QB3 is best. For if now 3 .... P—QB4; 4 P×QP, KP×P; 5 P×P will either win a Pawn or compel Black to weaken his position seriously in order to recover it.

The best line for the second player after 3 Kt—QB3 is 3 .... Kt—KB3, when 4 B—Kt5, B—K2; 5 P—K5, KKt—Q2; 6 B×B (note A), Q×B; 7 Q—Q2, O—O; 8 P—KB4, P—QB4; 9 Kt—B3, Kt—QB3; 10 O—O—O!, P—B3; 11 P×KBP, Q×P; 12 P—KKt3 (No. 48), maintains a small advantage for White because the Black Pawn position is weakened and exposed.

Note A. A popular alternative is 6 P—KR4! (Alekhine's Attack), the best answer to which is 6 .... P—KB3!. This line depends upon a number of complicated combinations and traps.

An alternative continuation for Black is to give up the center right away and play to get rid of the White QP. Thus: (1 P—K4, P—K3; 2 P—Q4, P—Q4; 3 Kt—QB3) 3 .... P×P; 4 Kt×P, Kt—Q2; 5 Kt—KB3, KKt—B3; 6 Kt×Ktch, Kt×Kt; 7 B—Q3, P—B4!; 8 P×P, B×P; 9 O—O, O—O; 10 B—KKt5. But even though he has neutralized the center, Black's game is not yet fully developed. He suffers from an endgame weakness (minority of Pawns on the Q-side) and his QB is still inadequately developed.

I. CARO-KANN DEFENSE (1 P—K4, P—QB3)

The basic idea underlying this defense is to get all the good features of the French without having to submit to the bad ones. I.e., Black

wants to nip any attack against his KB2 in the bud by placing a Pawn
at Q4 or K3, but does not wish to submit to a cramped position, and
in particular wishes to develop his QB. Nevertheless, the defense is
too passive and Black is compelled to concede White a lasting initiative.

The second moves are again practically compulsory for both sides:
2 P—Q4, P—Q4.

Now simple development will compel Black to give up the center,
after which White can retain his superiority by accurate play. Thus
the best continuation is 3 Kt—QB3, P×P (note A); 4 Kt×P, B—B4;
5 Kt—Kt3, B—Kt3; 6 P—KR4 (note B), P—KR3; 7 Kt—B3, Kt—
B3; 8 B—Q3, B×B; 9 Q×B, P—K3; 10 B—Q2, QKt—Q2; 11 O—O—
O, Q—B2; 12 K—Kt1! (note C), B—Q3; 13 Kt—K4, Kt×Kt;
14 Q×Kt (No. 49) and Black's position remains inferior.

Note A. Unlike the French Defense, Black cannot afford to wait
here. If 3 .... P—K3 we have a variation of the French Defense
where Black has thrown away a whole tempo by .... P—QB3, while
if 3 .... Kt—KB3; 4 P—K5, KKt—Q2; 5 P—B4, P—K3; 6 Kt—B3
and we again have a variation of the French where the defender has
wasted a move.

No. 49

Position reached in the Caro-Kann
Defense. White's game is preferable.

Note B. The object of this move
is to weaken the support of the
Black QB and thus compel the exchange two moves later. It is, of
course, inadvisable to exchange a
developed piece for an undeveloped
one, but the advance of the KRP
leaves Black no choice.

Note C. In order to avoid the
possible exchange of Black's Bishop
later. E.g., 12 P—B4, B—Q3;
13 Kt—K4, Kt×Kt; 14 Q×Kt,
Kt—B3; 15 Q—K2, B—B5! and
Black frees his game. If your opponent's position is cramped, do
not exchange pieces.

J. SICILIAN DEFENSE (1 P—K4, P—QB4)

The basic motif in the Sicilian is to create an unbalanced Pawn
position where Black will be able to attack on the Q-side, while White's
chances will lie on the K-side. It leads to complicated positions and is
less likely to end in a draw than any of the other defenses.

Best play is 1 P—K4, P—QB4; 2 Kt—KB3, Kt—QB3; 3 P—Q4,
P×P; 4 Kt×P, Kt—KB3 (note A); 5 Kt—QB3, P—Q3 (note B);

6 B—K2, P—KKt3; 7 Kt—Kt3 (note C), B—Kt2; 8 O—O, O—O;
9 B—K3, B—K3; 10 P—B4, Kt—QR4! and White's advantage is
minimal (No. 50).

Note A. It is essential for Black to prevent P—QB4, which would
not only ruin his counterplay on the Q-side but also prevent .... P—
Q4 once and for all.

Note B. The threat was Kt×Kt followed by P—K5, forcing
Black's Knight to an unfavorable square.

Note C. To prevent .... P—Q4, which would free Black's game.

No. 50   **No. 51**

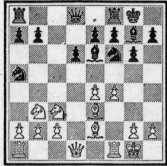

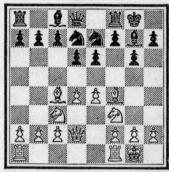

Position reached in the Sicilian Defense. White has a slight advantage.

Position reached against an irregular
defense. White's game is markedly
superior.

K. IRREGULAR DEFENSES (1 P—K4, P—KKt3)

The tendency to get away from the "books" and strike off on one's
own is widespread. Against a player who has memorized a lot of
standard lines such a policy is frequently successful chiefly because the
"book" player believes that anything that is unorthodox should result in immediate defeat. But this is just not so. If the opponent
opens irregularly the thing to do is to develop more quickly and obtain command of the center. Then, when one has the better position
and is adequately developed an attack may be begun.

The most effective way to proceed against the fianchetto defense
1 .... P—KKt3 is to set up all the pieces on their ideal squares.
Thus: 1 P—K4, P—KKt3; 2 P—Q4, B—Kt2; 3 Kt—QB3, P—Q3;
4 Kt—B3, Kt—Q2; 5 B—QB4, P—K3; 6 O—O, Kt—K2; 7 B—K4,
O—O; 8 Q—Q2 and White has a clear superiority (No. 51). This
type of development should be used against every irregular defense.

II. QUEEN PAWN OPENINGS

In the QP game White's ideal is again to set up a powerful Pawn center at Q4 and K4. This time he has his Pawn at Q4 so that the struggle will revolve about the attempt to play P—K4.

There are two ways to prevent P—K4: one is by a Pawn, the other by a piece. More specifically, the two best defenses are 1 .... P—Q4 and 1 .... Kt—KB3. White cannot hope to secure an advantage unless he plays his Pawn to QB4. For if he leaves the enemy center alone Black will be able to secure an almost perfect development in no time. E.g., 1 P—Q4, P—Q4; 2 Kt—KB3, Kt—KB3; 3 P—K3? (Colle System), B—B4; 4 B—Q3, P—K3; 5 O—O, B—Q3; 6 B×B, P×B; 7 Q—Q3, Q—Q2 and Black's game is perfect.

Of the myriad continuations after 1 P—Q4, P—Q4; 2 P—QB4, the Slav Defense, 2 .... P—QB3, avoids most of the difficulties and problems associated with other lines and is the one which we recommend.

A. SLAV DEFENSE (1 P—Q4, P—Q4; 2 P—QB4, P—QB3)

There are two basic ideas in the Slav Defense: one is the maintenance of Pawn equilibrium in the center; the other is the early development of the Queen's Bishop. It must not be supposed that both of these ideas can always be realized. Nevertheless, either one is sufficient for equality.

White has three main continuations against the Slav (See No. 52). The first is to exchange Pawns and rely on his speedier development. This is known as the Exchange Variation. The second is quick development with the idea of playing P—K4 at an early stage. The third is to compel Black to exchange QP for BP and then prepare P—K4.

In the Exchange Variation (3 P×P, P×P), it is not wise for Black to maintain the symmetry at all costs. In other words, now that equilibrium in the center has been established once and for all, he should not insist on an early development of the QB. Specifically, after the opening moves (from No. 52) 3 P×P, P×P; 4 Kt—QB3, Kt—QB3; 5 Kt—B3, Kt—B3; 6 B—B4, P—K3! is preferable to 6 .... B—B4. The latter move, while not directly bad, requires a knowledge of a number of complicated traps. But on 6 .... P—K3; 7 P—K3, B—Q3!; 8 B×B (note A), Q×B; 9 B—Q3, O—O; 10 O—O, B—Q2; 11 R—B1 (note B) the position is perfectly even (No. 53).

Note A. If 8 B—KKt5 (to avoid the exchange of Bishops), Q—Kt3!; 9 Q—Kt3, Kt—K5! gives Black the better game because White must lose still more time.

Note B. On 11 P—K4, P×P; 12 Kt×P, Kt×Kt; 13 B×Kt, P—KR3; Black's position is perfectly satisfactory because the White center Pawn is isolated and therefore exposed to attack. Besides, in view of Black's excellent development, it does not cramp the pieces in any way.

No. 52

Slav Defense.

No. 53

Position reached in the Slav Defense, Exchange Variation. The game is even.

The second line which White may choose is that where he leaves the status quo in the center untouched and concentrates upon the attempt to play P—K4. Here Black must develop his Bishop and prepare the counter-thrust .... P—K4.

This variation runs as follows, again beginning from No. 52: 3 Kt—KB3, Kt—KB3; 4 P—K3, B—B4; 5 Kt—B3, P—K3; 6 B—Q3, B×B (note A); 7 Q×B, QKt—Q2; 8 O—O, (note B), B—Q3; 9 P—K4, P×BP; 10 Q×P, P—K4; 11 B—Kt5, P—KR3 (note C); 12 B—R4, O—O; 13 QR—Q1, Q—B2 and Black has a good game. (No. 54)

Note A. Black must avoid the disruption of his Pawn position. If, e.g., 6 .... B—Q3?; 7 B×B, P×B; 8 P×P, P×P; 9 Q—Kt3 and White can exert a good deal of pressure.

Note B. If 8 P—K4, P×KP; 9 Kt×P, Kt×Kt; 10 Q×Kt, B—Kt5ch; 11 B—Q2, Q—R4 and Black has an easily even position.

Note C. A typical move in such positions, which serves two purposes. It not only compels the Black Bishop to stay on one diagonal, but also provides an eventual outlet for the King so that mating combinations are out of the question. For this point see also Ch. VII, No. 82.

The final position requires some elucidation. While White has two Pawns in the center to Black's one this is of minor significance here

Position reached in the Slav Defense.
Even game.

because Black has counter-threats against the White position. He will continue with .... QR—Q1 and KR—K1. On .... QR—Q1 Black would already have a threat: 14 .... P×P, and if 15 Q×QP, Kt—K4! for if then 16 B×Kt?, Kt×Ktch; 17 P×Kt, B×Pch, winning Black's Queen.

White's chances lie on the K-side, while Black should attempt to exchange as much as possible.

The third continuation for White is the most usual one. By developing both Knights immediately, the first player compels his opponent to give up his QP for the BP. If he can then succeed in forcing P—K4 under favorable circumstances he will secure an undeniable advantage, but Black has adequate counterplay.

Again using No. 52 as our starting point, this variation continues with 3 Kt—KB3, Kt—B3; 4 Kt—B3! The strength of this move (instead of 4 P—K3) lies in the fact that Black now must not play his Queen's Bishop out. For if 4 .... B—B4; 5 P×P, P×P; 6 Q—Kt3! wins for White. On 6 .... P—QKt3; 7 B—B4, P—K3; 8 Kt—QKt5, Kt—R3; 9 Q—R4, B—Kt5ch; 10 Kt—Q2 and Black is lost, for if 10 .... Q—B1; 11 Q×Kt!, Q×Q; 12 Kt—B7ch and 13 Kt×Q.

Consequently Black must reply 4 .... P×P (No. 55), when there are two main continuations.

I. 5 P—K3, B—B4; 6 B×P, P—K3; 7 O—O, QKt—Q2; 8 P—KR3 (note A), B—K2; 9 B—Q3 (note B), B×B; 10 Q×B, O—O; 11 P—K4, Q—B2; 12 B—Kt5, P—K4 with equality (compare No. 54).

Note A. To prevent .... B—KKt5. E.g., if at once 8 B—Q3, B—KKt5; 9 P—K4, P—K4 and Black's game is excellent.

Note B. On 9 Q—K2 (or 9 R—K1) Black must occupy the vital square by 9 .... Kt—K5. The advance P—K4 must be prevented as long as possible.

II. 5 P—QR4, B—B4; 6 Kt—K5 (to avoid the above equalizing lines and prepare a further strength-

Slav Defense. Position after Black's 4th move.

ening of the center position by P—B3 and P—K4), P—K3; 7 P—B3, B—QKt5!; 8 B—Kt5 (note A), P—KR3; 9 B×Kt, P×B; 10 Kt×P(B4), P—QB4; 11 P×P, Q×Qch; 12 R×Q, B—B7!; 13 R—B1, B—Kt6; 14 Kt—Q2; B×Kt; 15 R×B, B×P (No. 56) and White's hopes of an advantage are gone.

Note A. The Black defense is based on a complicated trap. If, namely, 8 P—K4?, B×P!; 9 P×B, Kt×P; 10 Q—B3, Q×P!; 11 Q×Pch, K—Q1; 12 B—Kt5ch, K—B1; 13 B×P, Kt×B; 14 Q×KtP, Q—K6ch; 15 K—Q1, R—Q1ch and Black should win. Only the possibility of this sacrifice, prevents the advance of White's KP.

Position reached in the Slav Defense.
Black has a satisfactory game.

Against untheoretical or just plain inferior continuations on White's part Black should react by an advance in the center. This principle, of course, applies to all openings. In the Slav Defense this center thrust consists of .... P—K4 at an appropriate moment.

For a long time it was believed that only actual and immediate occupation of the center by Black could offer an adequate defense. That is, after 1 P—Q4, P—Q4 was considered the only reasonable reply. After the World War, the upheaval in thought extended to chess as well and the Hypermodern School arose. One of the chief contributions of this school was the demonstration that it is in many cases possible to postpone occupation of the center by pawns. But the fundamental idea of the defense—the prevention of the strong White Pawn center with Pawns at K4 and Q4—remains the same. The differences between these hypermodern defenses and the classical ones are differences of technique, not of principle.

When the defense 1 P—Q4, Kt—KB3 first appeared, it seemed to be so ridiculous that nobody could figure out where it came from. Some wag proclaimed that it hailed from India, the home of all exotic and incomprehensible ideas. The name "Indian" took and has stuck to these openings ever since.

We have, first of all, the Nimzoindian Defense. The "Nimzo" part comes from Nimzovitch, one of the most original chess thinkers of all time, who popularized this opening. After the moves 1 P—Q4, Kt—KB3; 2 P—QB4, P—K3; 3 Kt—QB3, B—QKt5 (No. 57) we have the Nimzovitch position. There are no less than twelve fairly

No. 57

Nimzoindian Defense.

plausible replies, but we shall only consider the two most important ones.

In addition to preventing P—K4, the pin .... B—Kt5 has an aggressive purpose as well: to exchange at QB3 and weaken White's Pawn position. However, the control of the center is more important, and this weakening must not take place before Black has made sure that P—K4 will not be possible.

The simplest move for White is 4 P—K3, since he need not fear the doubling of his Pawns. Black's best continuation is 4 .... P—Q4! (note A); 5 B—Q3, O—O; 6 Kt—KB3 (note B), P—B4; 7 O—O, P×BP (note C); 8 B×BP, Kt—B3!; 9 P—QR3, B—R4; 10 Kt—K2 (note D), P×P; 11 Kt(K2)×P, Kt×Kt; 12 P×Kt (note E), Q—Q3 and Black stands well (No. 58).

Note A. This early advance is essential to prevent the establishment of a strong White Pawn center. If, e.g., 4 .... P—Q3?; 5 B—Q3, O—O; 6 KKt—K2, Kt—B3; 7 P—QR3, B×Ktch; 8 Kt×B, P—K4; 9 P—Q5 followed by P—K4, O—O, and White can proceed either on the K-side or on the Q-side.

Note B. An alternative is 6 KKt—K2, when Black should exchange in the center at an early stage: 6 KKt—K2, P—B4; 7 P—QR3, P×QP!; 8 KP×P, P×P!; 9 B×BP, B—Q3 with a good game.

Note C. This is necessary for else White will exchange and give Black a weak isolated Pawn in the center: 7 .... Kt—B3; 8 P×QP, KP×P; 9 P×P etc.

Note D. If 10 P×P, B×Kt; 11 P×B, Q×Q; 12 R×Q, Kt —K5, regaining the Pawn with an excellent position because White has a backward Pawn on an open file.

Note E. Or 12 Kt×Kt, P—K4 and Black will have no trouble completing his development.

Against the alternative 4 Q—B2 Black must also play for a quick liquidation of the center: 4 Q—B2, P—Q4; 5 P×P, Q×P!; 6 Kt—B3,

No. 58

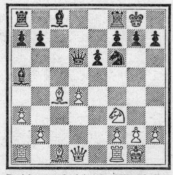

Position reached in the Nimzoindian Defense. Black stands well.

P—B4; 7 B—Q2 (note A), B×Kt;
8 B×B, P×P; 9 Kt×P, P—K4;
10 Kt—B3, Kt—B3; 11 R—Q1, Q
—B4; 12 P—K3, O—O; 13 B—K2,
B—Kt5 with an even position (No.
59).

No. 59

Note A. If 7 P—K3, O—O; 8 P
—QR3 Black secures equality by
8 .... B×Ktch; 9 P×B, P×P!;
10 BP×P, P—QKt3; 11 B—B4,
Q—B3; 12 B—Q3, Q×Q; 13 B×Q,
B—R3; 14 Kt—K5, QKt—Q2.

Against inferior play on Black's
part White will be able to force
P—K4 and build up a powerful
center, while if White plays weakly

Position reached in the Nimzoindian
Defense. The chances are even.

Black secures a strong attack by normal development and counterplay on the QB file.

Since White can avoid the Nimzoindian by playing his KKt out on
the third move, anyone who plays this defense must also be acquainted
with the Queen's Indian Defense. I.e., after 1 P—Q4, Kt—KB3;
2 P—QB4, P—K3; 3 Kt—KB3, P—QKt3 (No. 60). This fianchetto
is now possible only because there is no immediate threat of P—K4.

In order to challenge Black's control of the long diagonal White
should now play 4 P—KKt3. The best continuation for both sides is
then 4 .... B—Kt2; 5 B—Kt2, B—K2; 6 O—O, O—O; 7 Kt—B3,
Kt—K5! (note A); 8 Q—B2, Kt×Kt; 9 Q×Kt, P—KB4; 10 Kt—K1,
B×B; 11 Kt×B, B—B3 (No. 61) and Black's game is satisfactory.
The advance P—K4 has been prevented once and for all, while the
slight weakness in Black's Pawn structure is of no great importance.

No. 60

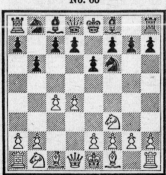

Queen's Indian Defense.

No. 61

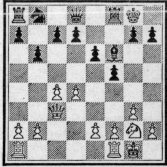

Position reached in the Queen's Indian
Defense. Black has equality.

Note A. Essential to challenge control of the vital central square. If 7 .... P—Q4; 8 Kt—K5 leads to an uncomfortable pin. E.g., 7 .... P—Q4; 8 Kt—K5, QKt—Q2; 9 P×P!, Kt×Kt?; 10 P—Q6!!, B×B; 11 P×B, Q×KP; 12 P×Kt, B×R; 13 P×Kt, Q×P; 14 Q×B and White wins.

Against weak play on White's part Black should occupy K5 and reinforce his piece there by .... P—KB4. In such cases, however, it is better to exchange the KB first. E.g., 4 P—K3 (instead of 4 P—KKt3), B—Kt5ch; 5 QKt—Q2, Kt—K5; 6 B—Q3, B—Kt2; 7 O—O, B×Kt; 8 B×B, P—KB4; with a good game.

III. OTHER OPENINGS

If White does not begin with the advance of either KP or QP, Black counters by placing one Pawn in the center, when he is assured of at least an even game.

The two most important debuts in this division are the English and the Reti.

A. ENGLISH OPENING (1 P—QB4)

This Pawn advance is at any rate near the center, so that White need never be afraid that he will not have an even game. Black should reply 1 .... P—K4, when speedy development will give him equality. The main variation is 1 P—QB4, P—K4; 2 Kt—QB3, Kt—KB3; 3 Kt—B3, Kt—B3; 4 P—KKt3 (note A), P—Q4; 5 P×P, Kt×P; 6 P—Q3, B—K2; 7 B—Kt2, Kt—Kt3 (note B); 8 O—O, O—O; 9 B—K3, B—KKt5; 10 Kt—QR4, Q—Q2 and Black's opening problem is solved (No. 62).

Note A. The alternative is 4 P—Q4, P×P; 5 Kt×P, B—Kt5; 6 B—Kt5, P—KR3; 7 B—R4, B×Ktch; 8 P×B, Kt—K4; 9 P—K3, P—Q3; 10 B—K2, Kt—Kt3 and Black has nothing to fear.

Note B. The loose position of the Knight might expose Black to a trap: if 7 .... O—O; 8 O—O, K—R1; 9 Kt×P, KKt×Kt; 10 Kt×Kt, Kt×Q; 11 Kt×Q, Kt×KtP; 12 Kt×KtP and wins.

On other defenses (such as 1 .... P—K3) there is the danger of transposition into less favorable variations of other openings. E.g., 1 P—QB4, P—K3; 2 Kt—KB3, P—Q4; 3 P—Q4 and we have the Orthodox Defense to the Queen's Gambit Declined.

B. RÉTI OPENING (1 Kt—KB3)

This opening is based on the idea of a double fianchetto and control rather than occupation of the center. The best defense for Black runs as follows: 1 Kt—KB3, P—Q4; 2 P—B4, P—QB3; 3 P—KKt3, Kt—B3; 4 B—Kt2, B—B4! (note A); 5 P—Kt3, QKt—Q2 (note B); 6 B—Kt2, P—K3; 7 O—O, B—Q3; 8 P—Q3, O—O; 9 QKt—Q2, P—K4!;

No. 62

No. 63

Position reached in the English opening. Black stands well.

Position reached in Réti's opening. Black's game is preferable.

10 P×P, P×P; 11 R—B1, Q—K2; 12 R—B2, P—QR4! and Black stands well. (No. 63).

Note A. The early development of this Bishop is important. On 4 .... P—K3?; 5 P—QKt3, B—Q3; 6 P—Q4 prevents .... P—K4 permanently, as a result of which the QB will be a constant problem.

Note B. Black is preparing the advance of his KP, which will give him a powerful center.

C. IRREGULAR OPENINGS

All such openings are met by an early advance in the center and quick development of the pieces. This will give Black at least equality; in most cases more. The play is no different from that in the Irregular Defenses to the KP openings except that the colors are reversed (see No. 51 and discussion).

PROBLEMS

No. 13

No. 14

Black's last move was 3 .... P—B3. Is this good or bad? How should White proceed?

Black just played 4 .... P—QR4. Why is this weak? How should White meet it?

No. 15

White's last move was 6 P—QR3.
What is Black's best reply?

No. 16

Black to play has only one good move.
What is it? What is the trap involved?

No. 17

This is known as the Classical Defense.
Suggest a good line for White.

No. 18

What happens on 11 .... Q—Q2?
11 .... Kt×KP is considered theoretically best. Can you see why?

No. 19

Black has just played 8 .... B—Q2.
What should White reply?

No. 20

This is the Lasker Defense to the Evans
Gambit. What is the idea behind it?

No. 21

In the French Defense White has played 3 P—K5. What should Black reply?

No. 22

Position in the Sicilian Defense. White to play. What is his best move?

No. 23

White has just played 3 B—Q2 in the Slav Defense. Why is this weak? What is Black's best answer?

No. 24

What is White's best move and why?

Chapter VI

AFTER THE OPENING, WHAT THEN?

TEN RULES FOR THE MIDDLE GAME

It is common to divide the game into three distinct parts: opening, middle game and endgame. The characteristic features of the opening are development and struggle for the center, of the middle game attack and defense, and of the endgame Pawn play and King activity. While the line between opening and middle game must always be rather tenuously drawn, we shall take it that the opening ends when most of the pieces have been developed. Moves 10–15 are usually the transition stage.

I. PLANNING

When a boy is thrown into the water to learn how to swim he begins by splashing about, jumping, pushing, kicking and getting his nose and ears full of water. Gradually he learns to control his movements, to kick only when he has to, to adjust himself to accomplishing his major objective, getting ahead in the water. How does he manag to acquire so much ease and control? Only by adapting each movement to the purpose which it is intended to serve.

The situation is much the same in chess. At first one flounders about, moves this piece and that, tries to get somewhere but can't manage it. Then one finds out how to control the moves, how to foresee what the opponent is trying to do, how to create threats and how to meet them. Further progress brings the ability to coordinate more moves, to make better combinations, play superior openings, produce more effective endgames. But throughout one progresses only by learning to play more and more *purposefully*.

We have already seen what the two major purposes in the opening should be: development and control of the center. The middle game is more difficult because these simple objectives have usually been reached, so that the problem becomes more complicated. Still, we have the all-important

FIRST RULE: HAVE ALL YOUR MOVES FIT INTO DEFINITE PLANS. DO NOT PLAY AIMLESSLY.

While this rule itself and the need for it are easily understood, it is essential to emphasize some general considerations before it can be satisfactorily applied.

A plan is made for a few moves only, not for the whole game. Very often people have the idea that masters foresee everything or nearly everything: that when they played P—R3 on the thirteenth move they foresaw that this would be needed to provide a loophole for the King after the complications twenty moves later, or even that when they play 1 P—K4 they do it with the idea of preventing Kt—Q4 on Black's twelfth turn. Or they feel that everything is mathematically calculated down to the smirk when the Queen's Rook Pawn queens one move ahead of the opponent's King's Knight's Pawn. All this is, of course, pure fantasy. The best course to follow is to note the major consequences for two moves, but to try to work out forced variations as far as they go. This means that many plans will be formulated and carried out during a game.

Plans are made for specific purposes only. Do not plan to mate him or to wallop him or to show him or to ruin him. Do not plan to capture most of his pieces or to weaken all of his Pawns. *Do* plan to weaken one Pawn, or to undermine the position of one piece, or to place one of your pieces on a square from which it will be highly effective, or to coordinate the action of your two Rooks, or to weaken the opponent's King position in some specific manner (e.g., by forcing his Pawn to Kt3 when you have control of the long diagonal).

Keep your plans flexible. Do not adhere to one hard and rigid series of moves which you are going to carry out cost what it may. Your plan should be composed of one central idea based on some sound general principles (e.g., weakening a Pawn and bringing pressure to bear upon it) and one or two short variations. It is folly to try to foresee everything and you can rest assured that nobody does.

The plan must be based on sound strategical principles. All such principles are given in this book and are based on the three fundamental ones of force, mobility and King safety. More specifically, this means that you must not make a plan which leaves you with weak or blocked or doubled Pawns, or which costs you material without adequate compensation, or which puts your King in an exposed position, or which deprives a vital spot of much-needed support, or which has one Rook biting on granite on the King's side and the other biting on steel on the Queen's side, while the Queen peacefully dozes in the center. Above all, always try to keep your pieces working together as one harmonious whole.

And finally, *the plan must be suggested by some feature in the position.*

A chess player is not a magician pulling rabbits out of an open game; he is a hunter following the trail which his dog marks out, the dog in this case, of course, being the position. This is why we can often have two plans working side by side—one long-range and one for only a few moves. E.g., the long-range plan may be to attack the enemy King position, while the shorter one may be to weaken the enemy Pawn position in order to facilitate the attack. All possible long-range plans, such as building up an attack, heading for the endgame, etc., will be given in this book. Short-term plans are based on immediate exploitation of some feature in the position. E.g., your opponent has a weak Pawn—the plan is then either to capture that Pawn or to bring pressure to bear upon it. The exact execution of this plan, and all the subsidiary plans which this execution may involve, will depend on where the Pawn is, what forces are available and what the situation is in other parts of the board. Or your Queen is blocking the development of your Bishop—the plan is to get the Queen out of the way. There is an open file tempting you—the plan is to take possession of it.

II. HOW TO ANALYZE A POSITION

The last point brings us to the steps which must be taken before a satisfactory plan can be formed. For if a plan comes out of what is on hand, the first requirement is the ability to analyze and judge a position. This is not, as some would have it, an innate gift, but a capacity based on definite knowledge and involving the answers to definite questions.

There are five elements in any situation on the chess board: force (or material), Pawn structure, degree of mobility of the pieces, King safety, and combinative possibilities. These factors give us the five basic questions:

1. Am I ahead, behind or even in material? (Material)
2. Are my Pawns well placed and how do they compare with my opponent's? (Pawn structure)
3. How much freedom of action do my pieces have, and is my degree of mobility greater than my opponent's? (Mobility)
4. Are the Kings safe or exposed to attack? (King safety)
5. What is the threat? (Combinations)

In all cases we go on to ask: What am I going to do about it?

The answers to these five questions will furnish a complete analysis of any position. However, in many cases one will automatically drop one or two either because they were answered the move before or because others are momentarily of greater importance. Thus if an attack against the King is begun, Pawn structure and mobility will have to take a back seat, while even material may be irrelevant. In attacks, combinations occupy first place and the fifth question is generally central.

1. MATERIAL

The basis for the discussion of this point was laid in Chapter III. According to our Principle of Force any material superiority confers a winning advantage. Consequently, if you are ahead in material you proceed on the theory that you have a won game.

Compensation for lost material consists either of better development or an attack against the King. In both cases the sting is taken out of the enemy counteraction by reducing the amount of wood on the board. This gives us our

SECOND RULE: WHEN YOU ARE AHEAD IN MATERIAL, EXCHANGE AS MANY PIECES AS POSSIBLE, ESPECIALLY QUEENS.

At first sight, this may come as somewhat of a surprise. Surely, you are inclined to believe, if I have more pieces than my opponent I am justified in beginning an all-out attack against his King. The trouble with this belief is that it underestimates the power of the defense. In chess, as in war, the attacking force must be considerably stronger to have any chance of success. As a result, if you stake all your cards on aggression, you are in effect nullifying your advantage, since the defense has a 50–50 chance of seeing it through. This is not to say that an attack must always fail. That too depends on the amount of material that one is ahead, and on the forces attacker and defender can muster. But the logical play is to exchange. By exchanging you will certainly win; any other course might win, but it also might lose.

The advantage of a piece or more is so great that it is customary for masters to resign as soon as they have lost so much. As a result it is impossible for the inexpert to obtain model examples of how to proceed in such cases. And yet the problem of how to win when he is a Rook or Knight ahead is frequently most pressing.

We saw in Chapter IV that the sacrifice of a piece must be based on a direct attack against the King. Barring blunders, this is the only thing that one must watch for. King attacks usually require two or three pieces. If one or two are exchanged, the danger of attack automatically disappears. This is especially true of Queens, for Her Majesty is the most powerful aggressor alive.

An example is seen in No. 64. White has sacrificed a piece for what appears to be a highly dangerous attack. On 1 .... P—KKt3, he ruins his opponent by 2 B×KtP, and if 2 .... P×B; 3 Q×Pch, K—R1; 4 Q—Kt7 mate. But there is a simple defense: 1 .... Q—R4ch!; 2 Q×Q, Kt×Q. The back of the attack has been broken. White will doubtless try 3 K—K2, when 3 .... B—Kt4! exchanges

No. 64

Black to play.

another piece and practically finishes poor White: 4 B×B, P×B; 5 R(R1)—KKt1, P—KKt3; 6 P—B4, K—Kt2 (note that with few pieces left the sacrifice at KKt6 is meaningless); 7 P—B5, R—R3. Now that everything has been exchanged but Rooks and the Kt, the problem for Black is no longer chiefly one of simplification, but of capture of further material. For once his King is in safety, he can concentrate his forces on any given point and, since he has more to start with than his opponent, he must win something. The technique to be used in this and similar positions will be given in Chapter VIII. For the time being the all-important principle must be grasped that with material ahead it is easiest to win in the endgame.

Blunders are one of the most common reasons for not turning a winning advantage to account. There is no simple rule to follow which will teach one to avoid them. However, if care is exercised, it will be found that they become more and more rare in your play. Before you move a piece see to it that there is nothing en prise. Examine the position of your opponent and determine what the ranges of action of his pieces are. The Queen is the most dangerous enemy, but the other men are on occasion just as effective. You must be on your guard against pieces which have penetrated your lines and try to get them out of the way as soon as possible. If one of your pieces strays far from home remember that it is more likely to be captured. A good way to improve your play in this respect is never to take back moves. If you make a blunder, pay the penalty—it will teach you to be more careful the next time.

With more than a piece to the good, it is usually possible to capture still more material by piling up on some weak point. With a Rook ahead a King attack is frequently justified and sometimes the quickest way to win.

Two Pawns present much the same problem as a piece: the only chance that the opponent has is an attack and a few exchanges will always nip it in the bud.

With one Pawn to the good the winning technique is rather difficult and even masters go astray. The superior side should proceed according to the regulation rules (full development, control of the center, avoiding Pawn weaknesses, etc.) and should be guided by the thought that every exchange brings him one step nearer his goal. However, unlike the other cases, here he must take care not to exchange too many Pawns. In particular he must always be careful to retain Pawns on both sides of the board. These points will also be considered in greater detail in the chapter on the endgame.

To the question, "What should I do about my advantage in material?" we now have a long-range plan available—exchange as much as possible.

A model example of how to apply this policy when one is a Kt ahead is the following game (Morphy-Pindar, 1859).

White: Morphy   Black: Pindar

(Remove White's Queen's Knight)

1	P—K4	P—Q4
2	P×P	Q×P
3	P—QB4	Q—Q1
4	P—Q4	P—K4!

A first-class Pawn sacrifice. If 5 P×P, B—Kt5ch; 6 B—Q2, B×Bch; 7 Q×B, Q×Qch; 8 K×Q, Kt—QB3; 9 P—B4, B—B4; 10 Kt—B3, O—O—Och; 11 K—B3, P—B3 and Black should have no trouble winning: he has a piece for one Pawn and is much better developed. It was not necessary to calculate this variation in detail: to foresee that White would have to exchange Queen and Bishop was enough. White's only hope lies in an attack.

5	B—Q3	B—Kt5ch
6	B—Q2	B×Bch
7	Q×B	Kt—QB3

Avoiding complications. 7 .... P×P is perfectly all right, but might lead to trouble.

8	Kt—K2	Kt—B3
9	P—Q5	Kt—Q5
10	Kt—Kt3	

Again White must lose time because he is compelled to avoid exchanges.

10	....	O—O
11	O—O	R—K1
12	QR—K1	Q—Q3
13	P—B4	P—B4
14	P×KP	R×P
15	R×R	Q×R
16	R—K1	Q—Q3
17	Q—Kt5	

With a great deal of effort Morphy has managed to conjure up some attacking possibilities, but since Black's King position is unweakened and he is adequately developed White's initiative soon peters out.

17	B—Q2
18 R—KB1	R—K1
19 P—Kt4	P—QKt3
20 Q—R4	

Threatening 20 R×Kt and if 20 .... Q×R; 21 Q×Pch. While even this would be meaningless Black takes the sting out of the sacrifice anyhow.

20	P—KR3
21 P×P	P×P
22 P—KR3	

If 22 B—Kt1, R—K6 and .... Q—K4. Once White exchanges Queens the ending is simple.

22	R—K6
23 Kt—K4	Kt×Kt
24 Q—Q8ch	

Desperation because the obvious 24 B×Kt simplifies too much: 24 B×Kt, Kt—K7ch; 25 K—B2, R×B!; 26 Q×R, Kt—Kt6; 27 Q—Q3, Kt×R; 28 K×Kt, Q—B5ch; 29 K—K2, B—B4; 30 Q—QKt3, Q—K5ch; 31 K—B2, Q—B7ch etc.

24	Q—B1
25 Q×B	R×B
26 R—K1	Kt—KB3
27 Q—B7	Kt—B4

Here Morphy resigned. Black will win most quickly by a direct attack against the White King (he is now two pieces ahead). E.g., 28 Q×RP, R—Q7; 29 P—QR4, Q—Q3; 30 P—R5, Q—Kt6 and mates soon.

If the material is even, the question of force is irrelevant for the time being and other considerations will precede.

2. PAWN STRUCTURE

The configuration of the Pawns is the most stable element in the position and must inevitably determine the course of the game.

Pawn play depends almost entirely on our Principle of Mobility. One set of Pawns is preferable to another if more moves can be made with it.

Now, the great strength of the Pawn lies in the fact that it can *promote* to a Queen. In order to promote, there must be no enemy Pawns blocking it, either on its own or the two adjoining files. Such a Pawn which cannot be stopped or captured by an enemy Pawn is known as a "passed" Pawn. It makes no difference whether there are pieces in the way or not. *Our basic principle is that the most valuable kind of Pawn is a passed Pawn.*

Normally Mobile Pawn Superiority

This theory is most applicable to pure Pawn positions, i.e., where there is nothing on the board but Kings and Pawns. It consequently assumes increasing importance as we approach the ending. In the middle game Pawns must also be considered as *targets* for the enemy pieces and *supports* for one's own.

Normally, if there are two Pawns vs. one a passed Pawn can be created by advancing and exchanging. E.g., in the subjoined diagram, we play P—Kt5, P—R5, P—Kt6 and if then ....P×P, P×P. This is how a Pawn majority should function. If there are more Pawns, the same maneuver is feasible: the extra Pawns counterbalance one another.

If a passed Pawn cannot be created by advancing and exchanging, the Pawn group is weak. For since two Pawns are held by one, or three by two, or four by three, one is in effect a Pawn behind.

There are three types of Pawn structures which are weak in this sense: doubled, isolated and blockaded (see Diagram No. 65). Doubled Pawns are worst, because they cannot even be dissolved by a sacrifice. Isolated and blockaded Pawns are temporarily stalled: a passed Pawn can be set up by giving up one of them. But the mere fact that they can only be made mobile by a sacrifice stamps them as inferior.

Besides these, we have Pawn structures that are relatively inferior: weak only because they are exploitable by pieces. These are of two kinds: backward Pawns on an open file, and "holes" in the King position.

A backward Pawn on an open file is one which cannot be defended by another Pawn, cannot advance and is exposed to attack on a file. Very often such a Pawn is so feeble that merely concentrating one's forces on it is enough to cause it to languish and die. Thus in No. 66 after 1 R—B2, R(K1)—QB1; 2 Q—R6, Q—Q2; 3 R(B1)—B1 the Pawn is attacked three times and can only be defended twice.

The configuration of the Pawns near the King is more complicated. The most essential consideration is that the King must not be subject to attack. He is safest when the three Pawns are on their original squares (67A). No. 67B is acceptable except for the case where Black can bring Q and B to bear on White's KR2. No. 67C is acceptable only as long as the B remains at KKt2. No. 67 D is inferior because of the mating possibilities at White's KKt2, and similarly No. 67E is dangerous because the Black squares (KKt3, KR2) can be occupied too easily by the enemy. No. 67F is not so good because the diagonal

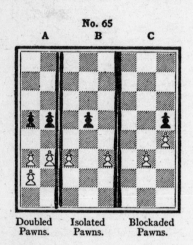

No. 65

A   B   C

Doubled   Isolated   Blockaded
Pawns.   Pawns.   Pawns.

No. 66

White to play wins a Pawn. Black's QBP is a backward Pawn on an open file and cannot be saved.

KKt1—QR7 is open and because a further weakening is too easily forced (Black can place B and Q on the diagonal KR2—QKt8). Nos. 67D and 67E are examples of "holes" in a Pawn position—squares which can be occupied by enemy pieces because the Pawns no longer control them. If all the Pawns are beyond the second rank the King position is inevitably weakened and the gap must be filled by pieces (67G, H and I).

No. 67. Pawn Position Near the King.

Excellent   Excellent   Good
A   B   C

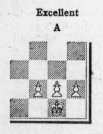

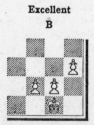

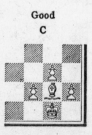

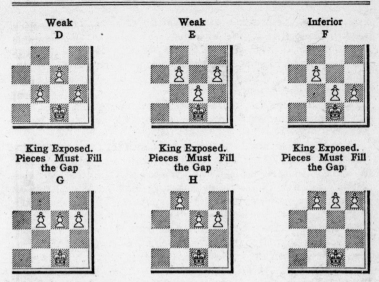

| Weak | Weak | Inferior |
| D | E | F |

King Exposed. Pieces Must Fill the Gap — G

King Exposed. Pieces Must Fill the Gap — H

King Exposed. Pieces Must Fill the Gap

Leaving the King to one side for the moment,[1] we can sum up the most important points in the

THIRD RULE: AVOID DOUBLED, ISOLATED AND BACKWARD PAWNS.

There are two other general considerations about Pawn positions which are worth emphasis.

No. 68A. Good.

No. 68B. Bad.

Black's Pawn position is normal and healthy.

Black's Pawns are weak because the QKtP is too far advanced.

[1] See Rule Five.

The first is the principle that *advanced Pawns tend to create weaknesses*. There are a number of reasons why this is so. Pawns should cooperate and defend one another. If one gets too far ahead of its fellows, it is apt to be gobbled up or to be unable to come to the aid of a companion. No. 68 is an illustration. In 68A Black's Pawns have made only one move. They have lots of reserve play and cannot be easily attacked. In 68B Black has no good moves and both Pawns are to be had for the asking. Remember that Pawns live by the motto: United we stand, divided we fall!

Pawns form the backbone of any position. Set them up well and you have a satisfactory basis for attack or defense, middle game or endgame. Set them up badly and you are saddled with a spineless jellyfish which is difficult to defend and affords inadequate support for any action that you may care to undertake. The reason for this is that Pawns, in addition to being members of the chess fraternity, play the part of ushers for the other members. They show the others to their seats, see to it that they keep their places, announce "Standing Room Only" when they are so minded. They are the watchdogs of the chess board. Technically, we express this fact by saying that *Pawns control squares*. This is one of their major functions in the middle game. And the more advanced they are, the fewer important squares they control.

As an example, consider the square KKt3 in White's position. When the game opens, this square is guarded by two Pawns, the KRP and the KBP. If neither of these is moved, Black cannot occupy the square. If the KRP is played, Black may under certain circumstances (B pinning the KBP) seize the square. E.g., in No. 69A Black's position is perfectly healthy and nothing can happen to it. But let him play P—KR3 and we get No. 69B where White wins at once by

No. 69A. Good.   No. 69B. Bad.

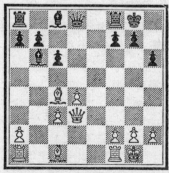

Even position.   White to play wins.

either Q—Kt6 or B×RP. On 1 Q—Kt6, Q—B3; 2 Q×Q, P×Q;
3 B×RP White wins a Pawn for nothing. Still stronger is 1 B×RP!
at once, for if 1 .... P×B; 2 Q—Kt6ch, K—R1; 3 Q×Pch, K—Kt1;
4 QR—K1, B—KB4; 5 R—K3, B—B2; 6 P—B4 and Black will soon
be mated, e.g., 6 .... Q—Q3; 7 R—Kt3ch, B—Kt3; 8 R×Bch,
Q×R; 9 Q×Qch, K—R1; 10 Q—R6ch, K—Kt1; 11 R—B3 and the
threat of a R check on the KKt file is disastrous.

When a square is not and cannot be controlled by any Pawn, it is
known as a "hole." The worst holes are those which immobilize a set
of Pawns. One type is seen in No. 67E. Holes in the center are of the
greatest importance in the middle game, which is why center Pawns
must be handled with care.

Nos. 70A and 70B illustrate sound and unsound Pawn positions.

No. 70A. Good.	No. 70B. Bad.

Even position.	White's Pawn structure is weak. There are two holes: at QKt3 and Q4.

In No. 70A the White Pawns are healthy because they are mobile,
while the square Q4 is under control. In 70B White's Pawns are
riddled with holes and in effect isolated from one another. Thus if
the QBP were threatened in No. 70B it could only be defended by a
piece. Black can occupy either hole, preferably with a Kt. The
QKtP is also a backward Pawn on an open file. P—QKt4 does not
help matters: Black replies .... P×P e.p., when the QRP is backward, and all the White Pawns are isolated from one another.

In the middle game holes such as those shown in No. 70B are most
effectively occupied by a Kt. Remember that a Knight is always
strongest in the center!

Again, remember that in general *Pawns in the center are more
valuable than those on a wing*. This point is, of course, in line with
the whole theory of the center.

It must be borne in mind that the last two principles enunciated are truest in the middle game, and diminish in importance as the number of pieces grows less, i.e., as we approach the endgame. This point is crucial when the question of transition to an endgame occurs.

Now we go back to where we started: What are we going to do about it?

First of all the Pawn structure determines two types of long-range plans. If the Pawns are *absolutely weak* (doubled, isolated, backward), head straight for the endgame. The technique of exploiting such Pawns is not difficult and will be given in Chapter VIII. This means that exchanges are favorable in such cases. But if the Pawns are only *relatively weak* (holes in King position, hole in center, too far advanced) stick to the middle game until a more decisive advantage is harvested.

Specific Pawn weaknesses always will suggest specific short plans. If there is a backward Pawn on an open file, the plan will be to bring pressure to bear on it, whether such pressure leads to speedy capture or not. If there is a hole in the center, the plan will be to rush a piece (preferably a Kt) there special delivery. If the Pawns guarding the King are weakened, the plan will be to undertake an attack based on those weaknesses. Similarly, if one is saddled with inferior Pawns, one should form plans designed to correct the inferiority. E.g., if one's Pawns are isolated, the plan will be to offer exchanges designed to connect them. Or if there is a backward Pawn on an open file, the plan will be to either exchange it or, if that is not feasible, to seek compensation elsewhere.

3. MOBILITY

Freedom of action or mobility is the basis of all position play. Where the material is even and the King safe, there is nothing else that we can go by, since Pawn structure is merely a special case of mobility. However, unlike force, it cannot be measured precisely. Still, for practical purposes the classifications greater (good), equal and less (bad) are quite satisfactory. If one has considerably less than the opponent (bad mobility) the position is said to be "cramped."

There are two features that must be considered in determining mobility: its quantity and its quality. Quantity is easiest—it is equivalent to the number of pieces adequately developed (frequently referred to as the element of time). This is of the utmost importance in the opening, where quick development is a necessity. In the middle game one should not be satisfied until all the pieces, or all but one, are off their original squares. In particular, one should try to have the Rooks connected.

The quality of mobility (often referred to as the element of space) depends on the kind of development, the control of the center, and the

degree of advancement of the pieces. Abnormal development represents a loss in mobility. E.g., a Kt at R3 is badly placed and decreases
one's total mobility. Similarly if one piece blocks another, or if a
Bishop is shut in behind a mass of Pawns. The control of the center
is the same in the middle game as in the opening. Finally, the degree
of advancement of the pieces can be gauged by the number of men on
and beyond the fourth rank. If White has his B at KKt5, while Black
has his at K2, with his Kt at KB3, other things being equal, White's
mobility is greater. Such a situation represents only a slight superiority. If, however, the White Knights are at K5 and QB5, White
Bishop at KKt5, White Queen at KR4, while Black's pieces are on
the first and second ranks, the plus in mobility is considerable and
White's advantage is proportionately greater. A word of caution:
The mere fact that a piece is well into enemy territory does not mean
anything; it must be able to maintain itself there for some time.

While the minor pieces are approximately equal in value, the mobility of the Bishop is frequently greater, especially in open positions.
For this reason one can assume that under normal circumstances the
B is a trifle better than the Kt. The strength of the Bishop lies in its
superior range, while that of the Knight derives from its ability to
cover all the squares. Two Bishops can cover all the squares just as
well, and consequently confer a tangible advantage.

Two typical cases of superior mobility are shown in the next two
diagrams.

In No. 71 White's Kt at K5 and B at KKt5 are thorns in Black's
side and guarantee White qualitatively superior mobility. No. 72 is
somewhat different: here it is not the White pieces, but the Pawns,
which cramp Black's freedom of action.

No. 71	No. 72

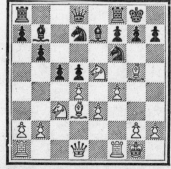 

| Black to play. White's position is su-perior because of his greater mobility. | White to play. White's position is su-perior because of his greater mobility. |

We can use these examples as a springboard to determine what to do about it in similar positions. In No. 71 White's advantage derives from the aggressive placement of his pieces. Consequently, if Black can exchange these pieces, he would almost automatically equalize. This stratagem is in point of fact always applicable; we can accordingly set up the

FOURTH RULE: IN CRAMPED POSITIONS FREE YOURSELF BY EXCHANGING.

As an example consider what would happen in No. 72 if all the pieces but the two Rooks and one Bishop apiece were removed. While White still retains a minimal advantage (open QB file, somewhat weak Black Pawns) it is no longer sufficient for a win. Or in No. 71: again remove everything but two R's and a B for each side. This time Black actually has the better of it because the White KP is backward on an open file.

No. 71A

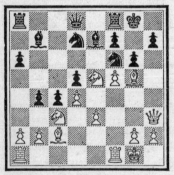

Position after Black's 5th move.

While it is always advisable to exchange pieces in cramped positions, it is frequently the only way to hold the game. E.g., in No. 71 Black blithely paid no attention to White's attacking possibilities and advanced on the Q-side. The result resembles justifiable homicide: 1 .... P—B5?; 2 B—B2, P—QR3; 3 Q—B3! (after this Black is definitely lost), P—Kt4; 4 Q—R3 (note A.), P—Kt3; 5 P—B5, P—Kt5 (see Diagram No. 71A); 6 P×P!!!, RP×P (note B.); 7 Q—R4!!, 2×Kt (note C.); 8 Kt×Kt, Q×Kt (note D.); 9 R×Kt!, P—R4 (note E.); 10 QR—KB1, R—R3; 11 B×P!!! (note F.), P×B; 12 R×Rch, B×R and White announced mate in six moves: 13 R×Bch, K×R; 14 Q—R8ch, K—B2; 15 Q—R7ch, K—B1; 16 Q×Q, R—R1; 17 B—R6ch, K—Kt1; 18 Q—Kt7 mate.

Note A. The threat is 5 Kt×Kt, Q×Kt; 6 B—B5, Q—Q3; 7 B×Kt, B×B; 8 Q×P mate. Black prevents this with his next move.

Note B. There is no adequate defense which does not cost Black a good deal of material. The major alternatives are:

I. 6 .... P×Kt; 7 B×Kt, Kt×B; 8 R×Kt!!, RP×P; 9 B×P!, P×B; 10 R×P mate.

II. 6 .... BP×P; 7 Q—K6ch, K—Kt2; 8 Kt×Kt, Q×Kt; 9 B×Ktch, B×B; 10 Q×Qch.

III. 6 .... BP×P; 7 Q—K6ch, K—Kt2; 8 Kt×Kt, P×Kt; 9 Kt×R, Q×Kt; 10 R×Kt, B×R; 11 R—KB1, B×B; 12 R×Q, R×R; 13 P×P. With Q+P vs. R+B White should have no trouble winning.

Note C. Or now 7 .... R—K1; 8 Kt×KtP!!, BP×Kt; 9 B×P and if

I. 9 .... Kt—B1; 10 B×R, P×Kt; 11 B×Kt, B×B; 12 R×B, Q×B; 13 Q—Kt5ch, K—R1; 14 R—R6ch, Kt—R2; 15 Q—B6ch, K—Kt1; 16 R—Kt6ch, Q×R; 17 Q×Qch and wins.

II. 9 .... P×Kt; 10 B×Kt, Kt×B; 11 R×Kt!, B×R; 12 Q—R7ch, K—B1; 13 Q—B7 mate.

Note D. Again Black has no choice: if 9 .... Kt×Kt; 10 B×B, Q—R4; 11 R—B3!, P×P; 12 R—Kt1, KR—K1; 13 R—R3 and mates in two: 13 .... Q—K8ch; 14 R×Q, P—B4; 15 Q—R7 mate.

Note E. Or 9 .... B×R; 10 B×B and Q—R8 mate cannot be stopped.

Note F. A brilliant conclusion. This is another example of how *an attacker should proceed by opening lines*, even at the cost of a sacrifice.

How could all this have been avoided? By exchanging and blocking the diagonal of the White KB. Thus in No. 71 the correct move is 1 .... Kt×Kt; 2 BP×Kt, Kt—K5; 3 B×B, Q×B; 4 Q—B2, P—B4! and Black's game is quite satisfactory. The method of freeing the game must be chosen with due regard to tactical possibilities, E.g., in No. 71, 1 .... Kt—K5 looks good, but is refuted by 2 B×B, Q×B; 3 B×Kt, P×B; 4 Kt×Kt, Q×Kt; 5 P×P, Q×Q; 6 KR×Q. P×P; 7 R—Q7 and Black has a bad position for the endgame because his Pawns are shattered and White's pieces are much more aggressively placed.

We have treated this case in such great detail because it is a beautiful example of how to exploit greater freedom of action by transforming it into an attack on the King.

According to our second fundamental principle (see Chapter III) superior mobility confers an advantage, but is not necessarily a forced win (as is plus in material). Consequently, the long-range plan which an advantage in space or time suggests is that it be transformed into a more tangible advantage at the earliest convenient moment. This is also clear when we realize that better development or more aggressive placement of the pieces cannot be maintained indefinitely, but disappears as soon as the opponent gets his men out or effects a few judicious exchanges.

There are only two really tangible advantages in chess: one is a strong attack on the enemy King, the other is winning material.

If, then, your pieces are better placed than your opponent's, you have one of two courses to choose from: either capture material or begin an attack against the enemy King. Since direct gain of material is often out of the question, the two motifs should be used together, i.e., combine an attack with threats of winning a piece or several Pawns.

In the continuation of No. 71 we saw one method of building up an attack. No. 72 is an illustration of a refined maneuver aimed at capturing material. It went on as follows: (begin from Diagram No. 72, p. 91). 1 Q—Q2 (note A.), P—R3; 2 P—R4, Kt—R2; 3 P—R5, Kt(B2)—Kt4; 4 Kt—R4, Kt—K5; 5 Q—Kt2, K—B2; 6 P—B3, Kt(K5)—Kt4; 7 P—Kt4!, P×P (note B.); 8 B—Kt6ch, K—Kt1; 9 P—B4!, Kt—B6 (note C.); 10 B×Ktch, R×B; 11 Kt—Kt6, B—Q1; 12 QR—B1! (note D.), B—K1; 13 K—Kt3, Q—KB2; 14 K×P, Kt—R5; 15 Kt×Kt, Q×RPch; 16 K—Kt3, Q—B2; 17 Kt—KB3 and wins. (For the technique of the win see Parts II, 1 and IV of this chapter and pages 160–166 of Chapter VIII).

Note A. Black was threatening to secure some air for his men by .... P—Kt4, which White hastens to prevent.

Note B. The alternative is 7 .... QR—KB1; 8 P×P, which gives up a Pawn for nothing.

Note C. As so often happens, Black does not choose the most promising defense in a difficult position. Relatively best was 9 .... Kt—B2, when he might still have held out for some time.

Note D. His plan is to capture the Kt by K—Kt3 and K×P. But first he wishes to forestall any counteraction on the QB file.

4. KING SAFETY

This, as we know, is one of the basic factors: it will frequently override all other considerations. The chief strategical point to remember is that the King must not be subjected to an attack by a large contingent of enemy forces. For this we have the

FIFTH RULE: DO NOT EXPOSE YOUR OWN KING WHILE THE QUEENS ARE STILL ON THE BOARD.

The term "expose" is equivalent to a serious weakening of the Pawn position, such as that in Nos. 67D, G, H or I.

This rule is usually only of negative value. If you keep your King well-defended, that ends the matter and permits you to turn your attention to other parts of the board. If, however, the King is not safe, the plan will be to fill up the gap or gaps with pieces, or to block the Pawn position in such a manner that the opponent will not be able to break through.

The reverse side of the rule is that if the opponent's King is not safe, the plan will be to attack him. We shall discuss the technique of attack and defense later.

5. COMBINATIONS

All that we have said up to now is essentially nothing but an elaboration of our three fundamental principles. But chess is not quite so simple—the factor which introduces all the complexity is the *combination*. A combination is a series of moves, all more or less forced, and frequently involving a material sacrifice, designed to effect some radical change in the position. This change will result in one of the two fundamental tangible advantages—material gain or King attack.

Combinations are what chiefly distinguish chess from other games and put it in a class by itself. They represent what Réti called "the triumph of mind over matter." They are unexpected, begin surprisingly, often consist of a series of pointless moves or even mistakes. They are literally the joining up of moves to form one whole and reach one objective. They are the poetry of the chess board, and their sheer beauty often blinds us to the merits of position play, which is the prose.

While combinations sometimes seem to defy the ordinary principles of chess, practically all obey one simple law, which is our

SIXTH RULE: ALL COMBINATIONS ARE BASED ON A DOUBLE ATTACK.

The reason for this is easily grasped. Suppose you threaten your opponent's Queen with your Knight. What will he do? Move it away. You have gained nothing. But now suppose that you threaten both his Queen and a Rook with your Knight. He can only move one of them, and must therefore lose the other. Or suppose we try to mate quickly by 1 P—K4, P—K4; 2 B—B4, Kt—QB3; 3 Q—R5 (hoping for 3 .... Kt—B3??; 4 Q×BP mate). Black repulses the attack by 3 .... P—KKt3, followed by .... Kt—KB3, B—Kt2 etc. But if Black had chosen a poor developing move, e.g., 1 P—K4, P—K4; 2 B—B4, B—K2??, then 3 Q—R5 threatens both Q×BP mate and Q×KP, so that Black must lose valuable material.

It is obvious that a double or simultaneous attack can be effective only if each branch is a *meaningful threat*. When are threats meaningful? Again in only one of two cases: where they result in mate, or in gain of material. Gain of material may be either quantitative, i.e., capturing a piece or Pawn for nothing, or qualitative, i.e., exchanging a piece of lower value for one of higher, e.g., a Knight for a Queen.

Ordinarily, as we know, the pieces will be working together harmoniously and the King will be safe. Consequently, we can assume that winning combinations are not possible if there are no *weaknesses* in the position. The two chief weaknesses are *exposed pieces* and an *inferior King position*. Where such a situation prevails, the air is combinative—we can expect something to burst. E.g., in No. 73 the Black King is attacked once (White Bishop bearing down on Black's KR2), while his Queen's Rook is wholly undefended. We look for a combination and are not surprised to find it there. 1 Q—K4!, with a view to both 2 Q—R7 mate and 2 Q×R is conclusive. Black must stop mate by either 1 .... P—Kt3 or 1 .... P—KB4, when 2 Q×R captures a Rook for nothing.

Our rule does not mean that a combination is nothing but a double threat. On the contrary, there is almost always something else in-

No. 73

White to play wins.

volved. But throughout the point to the combination which distinguishes it from any ordinary sequence of moves and enables it to gain essential time is this two-pronged coup.

Each element of the double attack must be a capture or the occupation of some vital square. This may be called the first degree of tactics: calculating and evaluating the direct powers of the men. Thus in No. 73 one part is Q×R, and the other is Q—R7 mate. These elements or simple captures can only be learned from experience. The reader will find that a little practise will give him enough facility to discern immediate threats and parry them.

The combination is the second degree of tactical play. In order to master it one must see the simple captures, but this alone is not enough. I.e., merely appreciating the fact that a Queen at K4 in No. 73 could capture the Rook will not suffice: it must be linked up with the mate at R7. Such linkings or combinations may seem confusing at first sight, but they fall into certain regular patterns which are reducible to a few for each piece. By familiarizing yourself with these patterns you will develop a "nose" for combinations and become adept at smoking them out whenever they arise.

THE COMBINATIVE POWERS OF THE PIECES

The easiest way to grasp the material here is to think of "combination in its literal sense, i.e., as "a joining together." Two advantageous directions in which the piece can move are united in such a way that one of them is bound to succeed. Thus we must consider the types of joining characteristic of each piece and the most effective focal points, i.e., the typical combinations and the squares from which they are carried out best.

1. THE PAWN

The lowly foot soldier is least useful for combinative purposes because its moves are so limited. No. 74 is the type case for the Pawn combination. It is clear that the Pawn must be attacking two pieces, so that one of them is bound to be lost. The Pawn itself must not be capturable. On the R file this straddle is impossible because capture in only one way is possible.

First Pattern for Pawn Combinations: Fork.

No. 74

White wins a piece.

Second Pattern for Pawn Combinations: Capture or Advance.

No. 75A

Black to play. White wins. Possible only on Rook file.

Second Pattern for Pawn Combinations: Capture or Advance.

No. 75B

Black to play. White wins.

No. 75C

Black to play. White wins.

When the Pawn approaches the eighth rank, promotion motifs create another kind of combination, shown in Nos. 75A—C. In 75A neither Kt can stop the P, for if 1 .... Kt(Kt2) any; 2 P—R7 and 3 P—R8=Q, while if 1 .... Kt—Kt4; 2 P×Kt! is conclusive. Note that Black's Kt at QKt2 is the direct cause of his downfall, for if it were somewhere else or even off the board, the P at R6 would have only one threat, an advance, which could then be stopped by 1 .... Kt—B1. No. 75A is exclusively the property of the R file: move the P to QKt6, the Black Kt to QB2, and the threat is quite adequately met by .... Kt—R3. But No. 75B, where the Pawn is on the seventh, may occur anywhere. If 1 .... Kt—Kt3; 2 P×Kt=Q, while if 1 .... Kt—Q3; 2 P—B8=Q. Again if the Kt at K1 is not where it is, the combination does not exist. Nos. 75A and 75B are not available with any other piece but a Knight. No. 75C illustrates the type combination with a Rook. Either 2 P×R=Q, or 2 P—Q8=Q will win at least the Rook. If the Rook were somewhere else on the first rank, 1 .... Kt—B2 would hold everything.

The essential elements in all three cases should be noted: these are the dynamic units which enhance the ordinary powers of the pieces.

2. THE KNIGHT

Combinations with this man are most properly called a *fork* (although we have used this term for other pieces as well), chiefly because neither of the morsels to be gobbled up can fight back.

The Kt must either attack two undefended men, or two men of higher value, or one man of higher value and one of lower in such a manner that the less valuable unit cannot be defended. More concretely, it should attack two undefended Pawns, or a Rook and a Queen, or give check and attack an undefended Bishop.

Nos. 76A and 76B show the general type of combination. In No. 76A both Rooks are defended, but one of them must bow to the Knight. In No. 76B one of the Pawns must fall. This kind of fork may occur anywhere on the board, but is most likely to take place in or near the center, for it is there that the horseman gallops most quickly.

The second pattern differs from the first in that a check is given, compelling the King to move. The Kt is peculiarly effective in this respect because there are only two answers when it gives check—capture or moving away, interposition being out of the question. The capturable unit must be either a Rook or Queen or wholly undefended.

The typical position where a Kt conquers a R on its original square is seen in No. 77A. The King must move, when Kt×R follows. An all-important point to be remembered here is that the Kt will not be able to escape after dining on the Rook: 1 .... K—Q1; 2 Kt×R, P—QKt3, followed by .... B—Kt2. This is why White does not win more than the exchange, or the exchange and a Pawn.

In No. 77B the Bishop is won for nothing. In view of the Pawn position, there is no danger that the Kt will not get out alive. E.g., 1 .... K—K2; 2 Kt×B, Q—Kt3; 3 Kt—R5, P—QB4; 4 B—K4, QR—QB1; 5 Q—B3 etc.

Often the piece which is en prise is not wholly exposed, but merely inadequately defended. In such cases one must count the number

First Pattern for Knight Combinations: Fork.

No. 76A   No. 76B

Black to play. White wins the exchange.   Black to play. White wins a Pawn.

Second Pattern for Knight Combinations: Check and Capture.

No. 77A   No. 77B

Black to play. White wins the exchange.   Black to play. White wins a piece.

No. 77C

Black to play. White wins a piece.

No. 77D

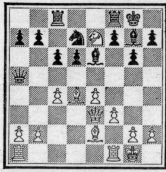

Black to play. White wins the exchange.

of attacking units, and the number of defenders, and must be certain that the defenders are outnumbered. Thus in No. 77C the Black Bishop is defended once (by the Kt) but attacked twice (by Kt and Q). Hence it must bow its proud head. This combination, incidentally, is one of the chief means of exploiting the weakness of Black's KB2. 77C arises after 1 P—Q4, P—Q4; 2 P—QB4, P×P; 3 Kt—KB3, P—QR3; 4 P—K3, B—Kt5; 5 B×P, Kt—KB3??; 6 B×Pch, K×B; 7 Kt—K5ch.

Once the King has castled on the K-side the points to watch are K7 and KB6. No. 77D is an example which is quite frequently engineered. The White Kt has just come from Q5.

Neither of the pieces threatened may be a Knight, for then the attacking unit is simply captured. Men which are separated by a distance of one or three squares on a rank (as in Nos. 76A and B, 77A and D) are subject to Kt forks. Similarly, men which can reach one another by one or three diagonal moves of one square each (e.g., White Rooks at Q4, K5, or Q4, KKt7, or Q4, KKt5) can be forked. Unless both pieces are on or near the edge of the board, there are often two squares from which the attack might be launched. E.g., in No. 77C the White Kt could produce the same threats if it were at KR6.

3. THE BISHOP

Here we can distinguish three major combinative patterns.

The first is that where two units are straddled. In this respect the Bishop does not differ from the Knight, except that its range is greater. The units must both be undefended, or both of greater value

[Rook or Queen) or one of greater value and unable to come to the aid of the other. No. 78A is an example of the last case. Since the exchange is a greater gain than a Pawn, Black will move his Rook and abandon the KRP to its fate.

In No. 78B the second eventuality is illustrated. Here the attacking piece is capturable, but defended. The Black Q must move, and the R goes. Instead of the White Rook at QB1, we might also have a P at QKt5 or a Kt at QKt4 or a Q at QR4.

This type of attack may be carried out from any square except the corners, but is again most likely in or near the center.

First Pattern for Bishop Combinations: Fork.

No. 78A

Black to play. White wins a Pawn.

No. 78B

Black to play. White wins the exchange.

Second Pattern for Bishop Combinations: Check and Capture.

No. 79A

Black to play. White wins a piece.

No. 79B

Black to play. White wins a Rook.

Third Pattern for Bishop Combinations: Pin.

No. 80A   No. 80B

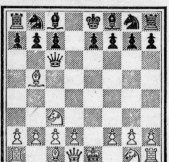   

Black to play. White wins a Queen for   Black to play. White wins a piece.
          a Bishop.

Secondly, we have various checking situations with the Bishop.
No. 79A once more has an exact analogue with a Kt (No. 77B). Black
must get out of check, and consequently has no time to save his Kt.

No. 79B illustrates the peculiar strength of the Bishop. This time
there is a direct attack on only one point, but a screened threat
against another. Since the screen is more important than what is
found inside, no effective resistance can be put up. The King must
move, when B×R decides. This last is the first Bishop type which
is available on any square of the board.

The third pattern is the pin, a stratagem which neither Kt nor P
can carry out. There is another subdivision here similar to that in
No. 79. In No. 80A there is a forced or *absolute pin*—the Q cannot
move (except to Q2) because it would expose the K to check. Consequently Her Majesty must abandon all hope. The B might also
be defended by a P at QR4 or a Q at K2 instead of the Kt. With
other pieces a variant on this idea occurs when the B pins a unit
which cannot be defended and accordingly must be lost. This is
shown in No. 80B. No. 80C, on the other hand, may be described as
an avoidable, or *relative pin*. Here the Kt has a number of moves,
but if it gets out of the way it will uncover the Rook. This is effective
when the piece being screened is a Rook or a Queen and the pinned
piece cannot be defended. By reversing the positions of the Kt and
the R we get a somewhat different situation. I.e., place Black's Kt
at QKt1 and his R at QB2. Again Black loses the exchange, but this
time because a strong piece is shielding a weak one. This is successful
only when the piece which is not directly under fire is undefended.

Nos. 80A, B and C may again occur anywhere on the board.

4. THE ROOK

Because of the greater power of the Rook there are no less than four patterns here. The first is the usual one of straddling or forking two units. When such units are threatened by a Rook, the combination leads to gain of material if both are undefended and cannot come to one another's aid, or if one is a Queen and cannot defend the other. This latter is the case in No. 81, where one of the two Bishops is lost. The typical possibility with a Queen and a piece may be seen by transforming No. 81 a bit. Place the Black Bishop at KB3, Black Queen at Q2, White Queen at QB2. Then the Black Queen must move and again a Bishop goes by the board.

This, as well as all other Rook combinations, may begin from any square.

The second pattern is new because it involves a mate threat for the first time. While similar situations with the minor pieces occur, they are extremely rare. In No. 82 Black is compelled to avert mate by 1 .... P—Kt3 or 1 .... K—B1, when 2 R×B nets White a whole piece.

The third pattern is the now familiar one of a simultaneous check and piece threat. As with the Bishop, there are two forms, depending on the relative positions of Rook, piece and King. In No. 83A the King must move, when the Kt will be captured. In No. 83B the King screens the loose Bishop. Since a check must be respected, His Majesty must get out of the way and look on helplessly while his adviser is destroyed. If the unit is defended in either 83A or 83B the combi-

Third Pattern for Bishop Combinations: Pin.

No. 80C

First Pattern for Rook Combinations: Fork.

No. 81

Black to play. White wins the exchange.

Black to play. White wins a piece.

Second Pattern for Rook Combinations: Mate Threat and Capture.

No. 82

Black to play. White wins a piece.

Third Pattern for Rook Combinations: Check and Capture.

No. 83A

Black to play. White wins a piece.

No. 83B

Black to play. White wins a piece.

Fourth Pattern for Rook Combinations: Pin.

No. 84A

Black to play. White wins a piece.

nation can be successful only if it is a Queen. In that event, White's Rook in No. 83A must not be en prise.

Next we again have the pin, but here there are four distinct varieties.

The first, seen in No. 84A, is the absolute pin of a strong piece, the analogue of No. 80B. The pinned unit may be either a Pawn, Bishop or Knight—it is, however, essential that no other piece can be brought up to defend it. Thus here the Bishop is a goner.

If the pinned piece is defended, the combination can be successful only if it is a Queen, for any other unit would be at least as valuable as the Rook. No. 84B is the type case for this branch. The Queen is lost, and Black can get at most a Rook for it.

Although Nos. 84A and B may occur anywhere, they are usually found on the K-file or the edge of the board.

The essence of the pin of a piece which screens the King is that it is illegal to move that piece, which is then as helpless as an ant stepped on by an elephant. We have called this an absolute pin. A relative pin with a Rook can be successful only against two minor pieces, or a minor piece and a Pawn, neither of which is defended, while the one directly attacked cannot be maintained where it is. In No. 84C, e.g., one Bishop must go because both are exposed and the one at QB7 cannot be held there. If the foremost unit is a Queen, as in No. 84D, the Rook must be defended, and the Queen must be unable to go to the aid of the piece behind it. Black has nothing better than some move such as 1 .... Q—Kt3, when 2 R×B is conclusive.

5. THE QUEEN

Since this is the most powerful piece, it stands to reason that there are combinations galore with it.

Although a Queen may move and capture either as a Bishop or as a Rook, this does not mean that all the patterns for those pieces may be taken over unchanged. The reason for the difference is that in many illustrations the combinations worked because Bishop or Rook captured a unit of higher value, but there is nothing capturable that is more valuable than the Queen. No prize is greater than the woman you love. As a result, the straddle of two units (Nos. 78A, B, 81) can be effective only if both units are undefended. This gives us Nos. 85A and B as examples of the first pattern for a Queen combination. But in addition we have the numerous cases where the Queen exerts threats in one direction as a Rook and in another as a Bishop. No. 85C is the type for this. Here the Rook must move, but cannot play to a square from which it holds the QKtP.

The second pattern is the same as that for a Rook—threats of mate and piece capture. Since the Queen can accomplish things in so many different ways, it is far more effective for this type of combination. No. 86A is the analogue of No. 82—the action of the Queen is the same as that of the Rook. Mate must be prevented, when Q×B wins a piece for nothing. The variant where the Queen threatens to capture material on one diagonal and to mate on another has already been seen in No. 73. Note that a Bishop would not have the same effect because checks at R7 would not be mate. Another common example of this pattern is that where one threat is on a rank (or file), while the other

Fourth Pattern for Rook Combinations: Pin.

No. 84B

Black to play. White wins the Queen for a Rook.

No. 84C

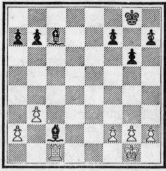

Black to play. White wins a piece.

First Pattern for Queen Combinations: Fork.

No. 84D

Black to play. White wins a piece.

No. 85A

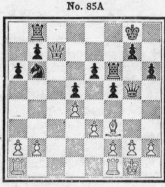

Black to play. White wins a piece.

First Pattern for Queen Combinations: Fork.

No. 85B

Black to play. White wins a piece.

No. 85C

Black to play. White wins a Pawn.

Second Pattern for Queen Combinations: Mate Threat and Capture.

No. 86A

No. 86B

Black to play.   White wins a piece.

Black to play.   White wins a piece.

Third Pattern for Queen Combinations: Check and Capture.

No. 87A

No. 87B

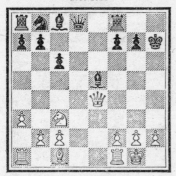

Black to play.   White wins a piece.

Black to play.   White wins a Rook.

Fourth Pattern for Queen Combinations: Pin.

No. 88A

No. 88B

Black to play.   White wins a piece.

Black to play.   White wins a Rook.

is on a diagonal. Thus in No. 86B Black must prevent mate at R7 and give up his King's Bishop: 1 .... Kt—B3 (or 1 .... P—KKt3); 2 Q×KB.

The motif of check plus capture can again be had with the Queen acting as a Rook or as a Bishop or as both. In Nos. 79A and 79B it makes no difference if the Bishop is replaced by a Queen; the same holds for 83A and 83B. However, in the general case with the Queen, the capturable piece must be wholly undefended. The greater value of the Queen appears only in positions such as Nos. 87A and B, where it checks as a Bishop and captures as a Rook or vice versa. In 87A, there follows 1 .... K—Kt1; 2 Q×B, while in 87B, 1 .... K—Kt1 (or 1 .... R—R3); 2 Q×Rch does the trick.

Finally, the pin, while possible, is much less effective with the Queen than with any other piece. For no unit of higher value can be pinned, except for the unusual case of a mate threat, and the enemy piece, which is attacked, must be undefended. The type positions where the Queen is successful are Nos. 88A and B. In No. 88A on any Knight move, Q—R8 is mate. In No. 88B the Rook can neither go away nor be held where it is. Nos. 84A and C also hold with a Queen instead of a Rook.

Queen combinations may also occur anywhere on the board.

6. THE KING

Since the safety of the King is so important, it stands to reason that few combinations with it as the main actor will be possible, and those only when the number of pieces on the board is small, i.e., in the ending. There is only one type—that where the King attacks two undefended units (usually Pawns) which cannot come to one another's aid.

Pattern for King Combinations.

No. 89A   No. 89B

Black to play. White wins a Pawn.   Black to play. White wins a Pawn.

No. 89A is the most common. On 1 .... K—B3 or 1 .... P—Q5, 2 K×P follows. Where a piece is involved, the most useful two units for combinative purposes are the Knight and the Pawn. Thus in No. 89B, the Knight must play and abandon the Pawn. The King can attack any piece but a Queen.

This sort of fork is possible anywhere except on the edges of the board.

Summary: This completes our exhaustive list of simple combinations with a single piece. If we analyze the illustrations and the principles behind them, we find that there are five basic types of double attack: 1) Forking two undefended units, or two units of higher value —this is a power which all pieces possess.

2) Checking and threatening an undefended piece or one of higher value—all pieces but the King.

3) Pinning an undefended piece—Bishop, Rook and Queen.

4) Attacking an undefended piece and threatening mate—Rook and Queen.

5) Threatening to capture or advance—Pawn.

Of course, many elaborations of these patterns are often encountered. E.g., it is possible to set up a position where a Queen will threaten to capture in six different ways. But all such situations are more easily mastered, and the problems they present more easily solved, when they are compared with the basic patterns.

In all the above cases only one unit at a time was involved. Naturally, there are also many positions where two pieces working together pool their forces, create a combination in restraint of the enemy. We shall call these *compound* combinations, in contrast to the others, which are *simple*.

7. COMPOUND COMBINATIONS

Barring accidents and coincidences, there are only three distinct types here—a pin, discovered check and discoveries in general. The "accidents" occur when one threat has been overlooked and another created. E.g., you can play P×Kt at a certain stage. Instead you attack the opponent's Queen with a Bishop on the other side of the board. Now you have a double threat, or a "combination," in the strict sense, but it is not something which could have come out of the position naturally. Sometimes these accidents, however, do come out of the position in a normal manner. E.g., if your opponent instead of defending a piece, counterattacks with another, by threatening the counterattacking piece you may be able to set up a twofold attack. No. 95 shows one way in which this might happen.

Joint threats with two men can be set up in one of two ways: one man holds the enemy down, while the other knocks him out (pin), or a man which is blocking the line of action of another man gets out of the way, and threatens something on its own hook (discovery). This last category is further subdivided because of the peculiar privileges and duties of the King.

a.) THE PIN

The effectiveness of a pin is due to the principle of mobility—the poor piece pinned must sit tight and suffer anything done to it because it is either against the law to get it out of the way or it has to sacrifice itself for more important units. This is why good players prefer to get out of a pin at the earliest convenient moment.

Once the unit is pinned, the idea is to attack it either with a man of lower value (P against a Kt, e.g.) or to threaten it at least once more than it can be defended. In both cases material is won.

Utilization of the absolute pin (where the unit has no legal move at all) is shown in No. 90. In 90A the Kt is held by the Rook and the Pawn delivers the kidney punch!: 1 .... B—K2; 2 P×Kt. In 90B the Rook is tied down by the Queen and knocked out by the Knight: 1 .... Kt—Kt1; 2 Kt×R. Finally, in 90C, we see how the combined efforts of two Rooks and a Bishop prevail against two Rooks. On 1 .... K—R2; 2 R×Kt, R×R; 3 R×R, R×R; 4 B×R White comes out a piece ahead. The principle in this and similar positions is that the number of attackers must be at least one more than the number of defenders.

The relative pin is usually effected when a minor piece is shielding an inadequately defended Rook or a Queen. If the piece behind is

Capturing a Pinned Piece. Absolute Pin.

No. 90A   No. 90B

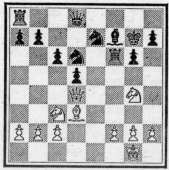

Black to play. White wins a piece.   Black to play. White wins the exchange.

Absolute Pin.

No. 90C

Relative Pin.

No. 91A

Black to play. White wins a piece.

Black to play. White wins a piece.

Relative Pin.

No. 91B

No. 91C

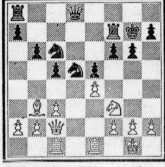

Black to play. White wins the exchange.

Black to play. White wins a piece.

undefined, either Rook or Queen will do as attacker; but if it is defended only a Rook can be successful.

In 91A the B cannot go away because it covers the Queen. So 1 .... Q—B3 is forced, when 2 P×B is decisive. In 91B Black should move his Kt because the exchange is less of a loss than a piece. After 1 .... Kt—B5; 2 B×R is, however, enough to win. 91C is different—here the Kt freezes to death because of a severe lumber shortage in the Black camp. Any Kt move would expose the Queen, so 1 .... Q—Q3; 2 B×Kt is necessary, with an easy win for White. Finally in 91D the Kt must sacrifice itself to avoid mate, for if e.g., 1 .... Kt—B2; 2

R—Kt8ch Black has to give up all his pieces and get mated into the bargain. 2 .... Kt—K1; 3 R×Ktch, R—B1; 4 R×R mate.

b.) DISCOVERED CHECK

This is one of the most destructive devices that anybody can think up—it is the dive-bomber of the chess board. For the piece which gets out of the way *may go anywhere it pleases* because it uncovers a check to which the opponent must give his undivided attention. Thus the discovering piece is free to do its darndest: it can capture anything, defended or undefended, occupy any square, guarded or unguarded. Usually the most effective stratagem is to capture as much material as possible, although on occasion a mating situation may be set up.

No. 92A is typical. The solution is 1 Kt—B6! dis ch. Now White's Kt is en prise to two Pawns and a Kt but is taboo because Black has to get out of check first. On 1 .... B—K2 or 1 .... Q—K2 there follows 2 Kt×Q.

A staggering illustration of the destructive force of a discovering Rook gone wild is No. 92B. Although White is a Queen and two pieces behind, when Black has regained consciousness after a series of hammer blows he will wake up with everything gone but a few old teeth. The correct sequence is 1 R×R dis ch, K—Kt1; 2 R—Kt7ch, K—R1 (unfortunately—or fortunately, depending on the point of view—forced); 3 R×Ktdis ch, K—Kt1; 4 R—Kt7ch, K—R1; 5 R×B dis ch, K—Kt1; 6 R—Kt7ch, K—R1; 7 R×P dis ch, K—Kt1; 8 R—Kt7ch, K—R1; 9 R×P dis ch, K—Kt1; 10 R—Kt7ch, K—R1; 11 R×P dis ch, K—Kt1; 12 R×Q and now that the shooting is over Black might as well give up. A mating situation could arise here if Black's KR2 were blocked. Thus if we place an extra Black Pawn at KR2 in No. 92B, White can mate in three: 1 R×R dis ch, K—Kt1; 2 R—Kt7ch, K—R1; 3 R—Kt6 dis ch mate. The Rook could also play to any other square on the Kt file in this final position.

Double check is a special case where the discoverer also gives check. Only one kind of reply is possible—moving the King—and consequently this device is chiefly useful for mating purposes.

A noteworthy feature is that either or both of the checking pieces may be en prise. No. 93A is striking. The solution is 1 B—B6! dbl ch and mate. Each check individually could be parried by a capture (.... Kt×B, ... B×R) or an interposition (.... B—Kt2, ... Q—R4). Yet because they occur together the Black King must move and, since he has no legal moves, he is done for.

A famous and important instance of the utilization of double check to lead to a mating position is No. 93B. Both Q and Kt are en prise and Black is threatening mate on his own hook. Yet White can win: 1 Kt—R6!! dbl ch, K—R1; 2 Q—Kt8ch!!!, R×Q; 3 Kt—B7 mate!!!!

Relative Pin.
No. 91D

Black to play. White wins a piece.

Discovered Check.
No. 92A

White to play wins the Black Queen
for a Knight.

Discovered Check.
No. 92B

White to play wins Queen, Rook,
Bishop, Knight and Three Pawns!!

Double Check.
No. 93A

White to play mates in one.

Philidor's Legacy.
No. 93B

White to play mates in three.

Discovery.
No. 94

White to play wins a piece.

c.) DISCOVERIES IN GENERAL

The principle here is the same as that for a discovered check: one of the attacks uncovered is far more vital than the other. As a result one threat is met, but only at the cost of neglecting the other. No. 94 is typical. 1 P—Q5! unleashes an attack on Black's Queen, which must move somewhere and allow 2 P×B. There must be a joining or combination involved here because either threat alone would lead to nothing.

Conclusion: What we have given are the fundamental elements to be found in all types of combinations. It goes almost without saying that many of the problems which come up in over-the-board play will not be equally simple nor have the exact form of our illustrations. But at any rate a solid foundation has been secured which will enable the reader to analyze the combinative possibilities in any given position.

It is helpful to think of tactical problems as a stepladder affair. The first rung consists of simple captures and additions of simple captures. E.g., a point is attacked four times and defended four times: then we know that it is safe. The second rung involves combinations with a single piece—a fairly exhaustive list of these has been given. Next we get combinations of the actions of two different pieces—the principles for this type have been set up. And finally we get the numberless elaborations and additions of the simpler elements, just as we have to climb up the lower rungs to get to the upper ones. In all cases the combinative feature arises when we do two things at the same time.

It is quite clear that in practically all our illustrations one or more Black pieces were weak or undefended or exposed to attack. This is no accident, but is always true. As a result, we can set up a valuable guide for practical play in the

SEVENTH RULE: IF YOUR OPPONENT HAS ONE OR MORE PIECES EXPOSED LOOK FOR A COMBINATION.

Nos. 95 and 96 are two typical combinative positions from actual play. In No. 95 1 P—Q5 discovers on Black's Q and attacks the Kt. The defense 1 .... Kt—K4 seems to meet both threats. But it creates a pin, which we try to exploit by 2 P—B4. Again Black has a way out for the time being: 2 .... Kt—B5!, a counter attack. Continuing, we find that 3 Q—K2 leaves Black without any further loopholes, for now both Q and Kt are en prise and the Q cannot defend the Kt (3 .... Q—QR3; 4 R×Q). Consequently Black must play 3 .... Q—KKt3, when 4 Q×Kt leaves White a piece ahead.

In No. 96 one should reason as follows. The exposed position of the Black Rook suggests the possibility of a combination. If we could place the White B at K4, remove Black's Kt from KB3 and his P from

Q4, the RP would then be inadequately defended. How can we get the Kt out of the way? By exchanging it for a White Kt at K4. How will a White Kt get to K4? By exchanging the Black QP. How will we exchange the Black QP? By setting up a Pawn at K4. But in each case the Black reply must be forced, for else he will be able to play either Rook or Pawn away. His replies will be forced in general

No. 95   No. 96

White to play wins a piece.   White to play wins a Pawn.

only if each intermediate step is a combination. Thus we are led to try 1 P—K4. This threatens P—K5, which would at present fork Q and Kt, but on a Q move attack the Kt and discover on the KRP. So there is no choice: 1 .... P×P. Now 2 Kt×P forks Q and Kt. If 2 .... Q—K3; 3 Kt×Ktch again discovers the attack of the B against the KRP. So 2 .... Kt×Kt is played, when 3 B×Kt finally gives us the desired combination (No. 78A).

The analysis of any position will lead us to one of three conclusions— that one side stands better, just as well, or worse than his opponent. This gives us a threefold classification—superior, even and inferior positions—and the rest of this chapter will be devoted to discussing the ideal continuations or most effective plans for each of the three cases.

IV. SUPERIOR POSITIONS

We must first of all determine what the superiority consists of. If it is material, we have already seen that one should head for the ending (second rule). If the opponent has an absolutely weak Pawn position, i.e., one which is a handicap under any circumstances (No. 65, third rule), again simplification, reduction to an ending is in order. But where the superiority is one of mobility of the pieces, or of a relatively better Pawn structure, then the thing to do is to *attack*.

You can look at it this way. A positional advantage is neither con-clusive nor permanent. The thing to do is to transform it into some-thing that is more tangible and more concrete, in other words, either to capture material or to get up a winning attack. Since winning material is the exception, attack must be the rule.

So far we have nothing new: the above is a short résumé of various points which have been mentioned previously. Here we shall there-fore confine ourselves to a discussion of the technique of the attack.

HOW TO ATTACK

The most important and decisive type of attack is that against the enemy King. It will either lead to mate or compel the opponent to give up a good deal of material as the lesser evil.

A King is most vulnerable when he is *exposed*. This is one of the chief reasons for the fifth rule. A King which is surrounded by Pawns and pieces cannot be approached and is consequently immune to direct attack. In order to be able to get to him one must open lines—files and diagonals—and train the heavy pieces upon weak and vulnerable points. Once more the analogy with war holds—before you can come to grips with the main body of the enemy's army you must break through the outer fortifications. We sum all this up in our

EIGHTH RULE: TO ATTACK THE KING YOU MUST OPEN A FILE (OR LESS OFTEN A DIAGONAL) TO GAIN ACCESS FOR YOUR HEAVY PIECES (QUEEN AND ROOKS).

Furthermore, the most useful files for the attack are the Kt and R files directly near the King.

The reason why the Pawn configurations shown in No. 67 are weak is that they either save the opponent the trouble of opening the lines (e.g., in 67D Black need only occupy the weakened diagonal with Q and B) or they facilitate entrance to the King position.

Ordinarily, lines can be opened only by Pawn advances. Now, since it is dangerous to advance the Pawns near the King (Rule Five) the person who intends to attack frequently castles on the other side of the board. He thus invites an attack because now the opponent need not be afraid to advance his Pawns. As a result a race to see who gets there first ensues and the decisive factors will be time and the number and kind of weaknesses each has.

If there are two or three Pawns in front of the King and they have not moved at all from their original squares, it is impossible to force an open file which would expose the King directly if the attacker has only two Pawns to advance. E.g., if the Pawn set-up is that in No. 97, White would have a powerful attack if he could open either Kt or R file, but he can only compel such an opening in 97B and C. For in 97A, if after 1 P—Kt5 and 2 P—R5, 3 P—Kt6, P—R3 and if 3 P—R6, P—Kt3 keeps the position blocked. But in 97B, after 1 P—Kt5 the threat 2 P—R5, opening the line for White's Rook, cannot be prevented.

With three Pawns vs. two, or three Pawns vs. three, an open file can always be forced by the sacrifice of one Pawn. Thus in No. 97C, 1 P—Kt6!, BP×P (or 1 .... P—R3; 2 P×Pch; or 1 .... P—B3; 2 P×Pch); 2 P—R6 clears the Rook file. However, this breach takes a long time to prepare and is not nearly as effective as that in B.

No. 97

A   B   C

White cannot open a file by Pawn advances.   White can open a file by Pawn advances.   White can force an open file by advancing his Pawns properly.

It should be noted that in such positions the gap may often be filled in by a piece. The defender's main object in life is to keep the position blocked; the attacker's to keep it open.

If the opponent has such an unweakened Pawn position, and blocks the heavy pieces, one must therefore try to weaken him by threats or sacrifices.

The sacrifice to expose the King position is an important stratagem and one which is frequently effective.

Once the King has castled on the K-side, the point KR2 is the one to watch. No. 98 illustrates the typical threat against this weak point. White wins by 1 B×Pch!, K×B; 2 Kt—Kt5ch and now if Black does not play 2 .... Q×Kt in desperation he has only three possible replies: I. 2 .... K—Kt1; 3 Q—R5, R—K1; 4 Q×Pch, K—R1; 5 Q—R5ch (or 5 R—B3), K—Kt1; 6 Q—R7ch, K—B1; 7 Q—R8ch, K—K2; 8 Q×P mate.

II. 2 .... K—R3; 3 Q—Kt4, P—B3 (or A.); 4 Q—R4ch, K—Kt3; 5 Q—R7 mate.

A. If 3 .... R—R1; 4 Kt×P ch and 5 Kt×Q.

III. 2 .... K—Kt3; 3 Q—Kt4 and now

a) 3 .... Q—K2; 4 Kt×KP dis ch, K—R3; 5 Q×Pch, K—R4; 6 Q—R7ch, K—Kt5; 7 Q—R3 mate.

No. 98

White to play wins.

b) 3 .... P—B4; 4 P×P e.p., Q×P (the best chance); 5 Kt (Kt5)—K4 dis ch, K—B2; 6 Kt×Q and wins without any trouble.

Black's best line is to decline the Grecian gift: 1 B×Pch, K—R1, but 2 B—B2 leaves him with a hopelessly weakened position. 2 Kt—Kt5 is not so good here (instead of 2 B—B2) because 2 .... P—Kt3 shuts in the Bishop.

This sacrifice can be successful only when Black is unable to cover his KR2 after the lines to his King have been opened.

However, the sacrifice can also be played to open the KR file for Queen and Rook. In that event White must be certain that the Black King will be unable to escape to the Q-side. The type position is shown in No. 99. Here there is no follow-up with the Kt feasible, but the possession of the open Rook file will be enough: 1 B×Pch, K×B; 2 Q—R5ch, K—Kt1; 3 R—B3. Black is helpless against the threat of R—R3; the only defense that can enable him to limp along for a

No. 99

White to play wins.

No. 100

White to play wins.

while is 3 .... Q×Kt, but after 4 R—R3, P—B3; 5 P×Q his game is obviously hopeless.

Sometimes the escape of the King is cut off by a Pawn instead of by a Knight. E.g., if the Black Q were at K2 instead of B2 in No. 99, with the Black Kt's at QKt3, QB3, White Kt at K3, and an extra White Pawn at KKt5, the sacrifice still works: 1 B×Pch!, K×B; 2 Q—R5ch, K—Kt1; 3 R—B3, P—B3 (or note A.); 4 P—Kt6 and Black is mated.

Note A. If 3 .... P—Kt3; 4 Q—R6, P—B4; 5 KtP×Pe.p., Q—R2; 6 Q—Kt5 and R—R3 will decide.

Where the point KR2 is defended, the sacrifice will work only if the Rook file is occupied and Black's King has no escape. An example is No. 100. 1 B×Pch! is conclusive, for if 1 .... Kt×B; 2 Q—R5 forces mate (2 .... Kt—B1; 3 Q—R8 mate, or 2 .... P—B3; 3 Q×Ktch, K—B1; 4 Q—R8 mate). In the last two examples it was not even possible to decline the sacrifice, for Q—R5 would have been equally devastating.

In many cases the sacrifice is the only way to make one's advantage count. E.g., in No. 100 on 1 Q—R5? the reply 1 .... P—B4! leaves Black with a slightly weakened, but nevertheless tenable game.

The open Rook file occupied by a Rook is a formidable attacking club aimed at the hostile King. No. 100 shows one way of utilizing it. Two other common continuations are seen in Nos. 101 and 102. In No. 101 White has no time to bring his Queen over to the Rook file, while Black is threatening to get out of his troubles by .... Kt×B or .... Kt—K5. But there is a simple continuation: 1 B—R7ch, K—R1; 2 B—Kt8 dis ch!!, K×B; 3 Q—R7 mate. Similarly, in No. 102, 1 R×Pch! is conclusive: 1 .... K×R; 2 Q—R5 mate, or 2 R—R1ch, K—Kt3; 3 Q—R5ch, K—B3; 4 Kt(Q2)—K4 mate.

No. 101	No. 102

White to play mates in three.	White to play mates in two.

All this leads us to a fundamental principle: if you are in possession of an open file and direct assault will not yield enough, a sacrifice to expose the enemy King will frequently be successful.

This is of greatest value for the KRP. The KKtP is less amenable to sacrifices because normally there is no piece that can be trained on it (as a B at Q3 eyes the enemy KRP). Once the KKt file is open, No. 103A is a basic mating position. On 1 P—B6, P—Kt3; 2 Q—R6, mate next cannot be avoided.

No. 103A

White to play mates in three.

With the White Pawn at B6, Black Pawn at KKt3, and square KKt2 undefended, if White can succeed in getting his Q to KR6 he will have a devastating attack. An illustration is No. 103B, where White has given up a piece and a Pawn. But 1 Q—K3! is conclusive: 1 .... K—R1 (Note A.); 2 Q—R 6, R—Kt1; 3 R—B3 (threatening R—R3), Q—KB1; 4 Q×Pch!, K×Q; 5 R—R3ch, Q—R3; 6 R×Q mate. Note A. Essential to stop Q—R6 and Q—Kt7 mate. If 1 .... Kt×P; 2 Q—R6, Q×P; 3 R×Q Black's game is hopeless.

With an open diagonal (defending Pawns at KB2, KKt3, KR2) which is not occupied by a piece, the aggressor should try to seize it with Queen and Bishop. Such a diagonal must be blocked by the defender at all costs. What happens if he does not do so is seen in No. 104. Black is two Pawns ahead, but the weakening of his King posi-

No. 103B

White to play wins.

No. 104

White to play wins.

tion is fatal: 1 Q—K5!, P—KB3; 2 R×P, R×R (Note A.); 3 Q×R, Q—Q2; 4 Q—R8ch, K—B2; 5 R—B1ch, K—K2; 6 Q—B8 mate.

Note A. Or 2 .... Q—Q2; 3 R(Kt1)—KB1, Kt—B3; 4 R×Rch, R×R; 5 Q—R8 mate.

In this and similar positions the critical diagonal can often most effectively be exploited by a sacrifice. Thus in No. 105 Black plays 1 .... Q—B6! first. This threatens to win a piece by either .... B or R×Kt, since the QP is pinned. E.g., 2 QR—K1, R×Kt. So 2 Q—Kt2 is as good as forced. Now 2 .... B×Kt; 3 P×B, Q×KP would only win a measly Pawn. Instead 2 .... R×Kt! mates: 3 P—B4,

No. 105

Black to play wins.

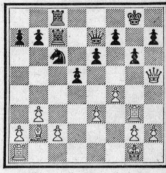

No. 106

White to play mates in four.

R×P!! (uncovering the B diagonal and defending the B) and mate at KKt7 cannot be prevented.

Another typical example is No. 106. If White dilly-dallies, ... P—B3 will block the diagonal of the B and leave Black with a playable game. Instead 1 Q×RPch!! lifts Black out of his seat: 1 .... K×Q; 2 R—R3ch, Q—R5; 3 R×Qch, K—Kt1; 4 R—R8 mate.

Once the Pawns have been weakened by moving up, the thing to do is to exchange the most advanced Pawn, taking care to avoid a blockade, which is always a pail of cold water on the attacker's head.

Against a Pawn at Kt3, the idea is to play the RP up to R5, making sure that the reply .... P—KKt4 is not available, and then concentrate forces on the open KR file. No. 107, from a game Steinitz*-Tchigorin, is typical. Although White has no appreciable superiority in mobility, the attack proves successful because of the relative safety

*Wilhelm Steinitz, 1836–1900, was champion of the world from 1866 until 1894. He was the first to expound the theory of correct positional chess.

No. 107

No. 108

White to play. Position after Black's
10th move.

White to play. Position after Black's
15th move.

of his King (which will go to the Q-side). The game continued:

| 11 P—KR4 | Kt—K2 |
| 12 P—R5! | |

Ordinarily it would be necessary to block the KtP, but here this is
not essential because 12 .... P—KKt4 can be answered by 13 P—R6,
B—R1; 14 Kt—B5, forcing .... P—B3, which would stalemate
Black's KB completely.

| 12 .... | P—Q4 |

The proper reply: counter an attack on the wing by a thrust in the
center.

| 13 RP×P | BP×P? |

This, however, is a fatal mistake because it does not block the R file
effectively and opens the diagonal to White's King's Bishop. 13
.... RP×P, followed by .... P—B3, allowing the King to escape to
the Q-side, was preferable. On general principles, *never open new lines
to your opponent if you are defending.*

14 P×P	Kt×P
15 Kt×Kt	Q×Kt
16 B—Kt3	Q—B3
17 Q—K2	B—Q2
18 B—K3	K—R1
19 O—O—O	QR—K1

Black is already in a bad way. If 19 .... Kt—B4; 20 R×Pch!
(compare No. 102), K×R; 21 Kt—Kt5ch, K—R1; 22 R—R1ch, B --

R3; 23 R×Bch, K—Kt2; 24 R—R7ch, K—B3; 25 Kt—K4ch, Kt×
Kt; 26 P×Kt and Black will have to give up at least a piece to get out
of the mating net.

20 Q—B1	P—QR4
21 P—Q4	

The attacker always tries to keep the game as open as possible.

21	P×P
22 Kt×P	B×Kt
23 R×B!!	Kt×R

On other moves 24 R(Q4)—KR4 would win quickly.

24 R×Pch!!!	K×R
25 Q—R1ch	K—Kt2
26 B—R6ch	K—B3
27 Q—R4ch	K—K4
28 Q×Ktch	Resigns

Too early! 28 .... K—B4; 29 P—Kt4 mate was a more fitting
conclusion.

When Black has weakened his position by playing his RP to R3,
the thing to do is to advance the KKtP and open the file in that manner. Frequently an open diagonal, however, will prove to be more important than a file. Do not stick to one line rigidly: remember that
the idea is to get at his King and take advantage of whatever opportunity turns up.

No. 108 is an excellent example of the technique and the situations
that arise. White has an advantage in mobility—his Bishops are more
aggressively placed than those of his opponent, while his Knight occupies a strong central post. He will try to utilize this advantage by
building up an attack. Consequently an advance on the K-side is in
order. Black's chances lie on the Q-side, but he is much less likely to
succeed because there is no weakness in the White Pawn position,
while the Black KRP is a natural target.

We shall follow the game continuation:

16 P—KKt4	Kt(B3)—Q2
17 P—KR4!	

Such Pawn sacrifices are common. Black does not dare to open the
gates and let White's heavy pieces in. E.g., 17 .... B×P; 18 Q—R2,
B—Kt4; 19 B×B, Q×B; 20 P—B4, Q—K2; 21 P—Kt5, Kt×Kt;
22 BP×Kt!, P—Kt5; 23 Kt—K2, Kt—B5; 24 P×P, P—Kt3 (else
25 P×P will lead to a speedy mate); 25 P—R7ch, K—R1; 26 Kt—B4,

QR—B1; 27 B×P!, P—R4; 28 QR—Kt1, R—B3; 29 B×P!, Q×B;
30 R—Kt8ch, R×R; 31 P×R=Q dbl ch, K×Q; 32 Q—R8 mate.

Another possibility here is 17 .... B×P; 18 Q—R2, P—Kt4;
(instead of .... B—Kt4); 19 B—Kt3, Kt×Kt; 20 P×Kt, P—Kt5;
21 B×B, P×B; 22 P—Kt5!!, P×P; 23 QR—Kt1, K—R1; 24 P—B4,
P×Kt; 25 R×P and will mate in a few.

17 ....   R—B1
18 P—Kt5!

Time is of the essence in an attack and all non-essentials must be set
to one side. If in reply 18 .... P—Kt5; 19 P×P, P×Kt; 20 Q—Kt2,
B—KB3; 21 P×P, R—K1; 22 P—R5, Kt×Kt; 23 P—R6!!, Kt—
Kt3; 24 B×Kt, P×B; 25 Q×P, P—B7ch; 26 K—R1, P×R=Qch;
27 R×Q and if 27 .... B×P; 28 Q×B mate, while on any other reply
28 P—R7 is mate.

18 ....   P—KR4
(see diagram)

No. 108A

Position after Black's 18th move.

19 P—Kt6!

The Pawn at KR4 must always
be cut off from any possible Pawn
support.

19 ....   P—Kt5

Or 19 .... P—B3; 20 Kt×Kt,
Kt×Kt; 21 B—B5, R—B3; 22
R(Q1)—K1, R—K1; 23 B—K6ch,
R×B; 24 R×R, Kt—B1; 25 R—
K2. Now White is the exchange
ahead, while his attack has lost
little of its vigor.

20 P×Pch   R×P

If 20 .... K—R1; 21 Kt—Kt6ch, K—R2 the discovered checks
will net White a gold mine: 22 Kt×R dbl ch, K—R1; 23 Kt—Kt6ch,
K—R2; 24 Kt×B dis ch, K—R1; 25 Kt—Kt6ch, K—R2; 26 P—
B8=Q, Kt×Q; 27 Kt×Kt dbl ch, etc.

21 B—R7ch   K—B1
22 Kt×R   K×Kt
23 Q—Kt6ch   K—B1
24 Q—K6!   Resigns

The only move to ward off mate is 24 .... Kt—B3, when 25 B—
Kt6! compels Black to give up his Queen.

With Pawns that are otherwise weakened the principle is always the same—open the files for the heavy pieces. Nos. 109 and 110 illustrate two other important cases. Both are particularly instructive because the attack was conducted perfectly.

No. 109

No. 110

Position after Black's 10th move.
White will open the KKt file.

Position after Black's 17th move.
White will open a file on the K-side.

In No. 109 White is going to try to open the KKt file. On 1 P—KKt4 directly, the reply 1 .... P—B5! still leaves the line blocked. So White will first make sure that the BP will not be able to advance and will then concentrate his forces on the Black King position.

The game continued:

11 P—B4	B×P
12 P—KKt4	P×P
13 Q—Kt3!	

Not 13 Q×KtP?, B—K6ch and .... R or B×P. The temporary sacrifice of the Pawn is of no moment.

13	Q—R4

Black attempts to create a counterattack, but is unsuccessful because there are no weaknesses in the White King position.

14 K—Kt1	B—Kt5
15 Kt(B3)—K2	Kt—K2
16 Kt—Q4	B—B4

It would never do for Black to try to hold the extra Pawn by .... P—KR4 at any stage, for the reply P—KR3 would then open two files (KKt and KR) instead of one.

17 Kt—Kt3	Q—Kt3
18 Kt×B	Q×Kt
19 B—Q3	Kt—B4
20 Q×P!!	P—KKt3

If 20 .... Kt—K6; 21 Q—R5!, P—KKt3; 22 B×P, P×B; 23 Q×
Pch, K—R1; 24 R—QB1, Q—B2; 25 Q—R6ch, K—Kt1; 26 Kt—B3
with an easy win, e.g., 26 .... Kt—B4; 27 KR—Kt1ch, K—B2; 28
Q—R7ch, K—K1; 29 Q×Q, etc.

21 Kt—R3!

He need not lose time to defend the Rook, as the sequel shows.

21	Kt—K6

Playing for a desperate counterattack. The more quiet 21 ....
B—Q2; 22 Kt—Kt5, QR—B1; 23 Q—R3, P—KR4; 24 KR—Kt1 is,
however, also untenable in the long run.

22 Q—Kt1!	Q—Kt3
(see diagram)	

No. 109A

White to play wins.

Releasing the pin and threatening .... Kt×R. But there is an
unpleasant surprise in store for
him.

23 B×P!!

A typical sacrifice to deprive the
King of all Pawn support.

23	Kt×R

Or 23 .... P×B; 24 Q×Pch,
K—R1; 25 KR—Kt1, Q—B2; 26
Q—R6ch, Q—R2; 27 Q×Rch, Q—
Kt1; 28 Q×Q mate.

24 B×P dbl ch!!!	K×B

Forced, for if 24 .... K—B2, simply 25 Q—Kt6ch, K—K2; 26
R×Kt leaves White with two Pawns for the exchange and an attack
which is just as strong as ever.

25 Q×Kt	R—B4
26 R—Kt1	B—Q2
27 Q—Kt4	Q×Rch

The only way to stop mate.

28 Q×Q	R—KKt1
29 Q×P	

With Q+3P's vs. 2 R's the rest is not difficult. The guiding idea is that by advancing his Pawns White will compel Black to give up more material to stop them from queening.

29	B—B3
30 P—Kt4	P—Q5
31 Kt—Kt5ch	R(Kt)×Kt
32 P×R	R×KP
33 P—KR4	R—K5
34 Q—B5	K—Kt3
35 Q—B8	R×P
36 Q—B6ch	K—R4
37 P—Kt6	P—Q6
38 Q—R8ch	K—Kt4
39 P—Kt7!	Resigns.

In No. 110 White will crash through Black's game by concentrating on the Black KRP. The continuation was:

18 B—K2	Q—B2
19 R—Q2!	

The threat was 19 .... Kt—K5.

19	B—K1
20 P—KKt4!	P×P

It makes no difference whether Black exchanges or not. If, e.g., 20 .... K—K2; 21 P×P, P×P; 22 P—B5 opens more lines.

21 B×KtP	R—Q1
22 P—R5	

The attacker should keep the game as open as possible.

22	Q—Kt3
23 P×P	R×R
24 B×R	P×P
25 B×P!	Q—R4

There is nothing better. On 25 .... Q×B; 26 Q×Ktch and 27 Kt×P would follow.

26 P—B5

It is always advisable to continue the attack as long as possible. Transition to an ending should not be allowed until one is at least the exchange ahead.

26	Kt×B
27 P×Kt	Q—B2
28 Q—B4ch	K—Kt1
29 Kt×P	R×Kt

Desperation. If 29 .... Q—R4; 30 Kt—K7ch, K—Kt2; 31 Q—B6ch, K—R3; 32 R—R2 mate.

30 R×R	Q—B3
31 R—Q6	Q—R5
32 Q×Q	B×Q
33 R—Q7!	Resigns.

White has too many Pawns. After 33 .... B×R; 34 P×B, one Pawn queens. On other moves White will capture more Pawns and eventually the Black Bishop.

Against a King which has castled on the Queen's wing the same type of Pawn advance should be adopted. It is as a rule easier to attack a King which has castled long because there is more terrain to defend.

The sacrifice of a piece to expose the enemy King is a device which has been noted time and again. It is frequently one of the most serious threats that the attacker has and in superior positions one should always be on the lookout for possibilities of such offers. Two more common cases where this kind of sacrifice is conclusive are shown in Nos. 111 and 112.

No. 111

White to play wins.

No. 112

White to play mates in two.

In No. 111 the move is 1 B×P!, P×B (Black's best chance is to let matters stand, but with a Pawn behind his game is then theoretically lost); 2 Q×P, R—K1 (the only way to stop Q—R7 mate); 3 B—R7ch, K—R1; 4 R×B!!, R×R; 5 B—Kt6 dis ch, K—Kt1; 6 Q—R7ch, K—B1; 7 Q×P mate.

The combination in No. 112 is 1 Q×Pch!!, P×Q; 2 B—R6 mate. This comes up only when Black has castled on the Queen's side.

All the above examples help to clarify the technique of an attack on the King, where the immediate objective is to secure mate or a considerable material advantage. If the King is not directly involved, similar Pawn play will be aimed at weakening of the enemy Pawn structure or penetration to the seventh rank with a Rook.

No. 113

White to play.

No. 114

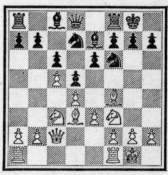

White to play.

No. 113 is typical. White has the more aggressive Pawn position, but must not be content unless he can convert this into a more tangible superiority. With this in mind he plays 1 P—QKt4, to continue with P—B5, KR—B1, etc. E.g., 1 P—QKt4, B—Kt2; 2 P—B5, KtP×P (Note A.); 3 P×P, P×P (Note B.); 4 B×P and Black is saddled with a backward Pawn on an open file.

Note A. If 2 .... R—B1; 3 P—B6, B—R1; 4 Q—R4, winning the RP.

Note B. Or 3 .... Kt—K1; 4 Kt—B4, P—Kt3; 5 Kt—R5, R—Kt1; 6 P—B6, B—R1; 7 B×P and again Black has lost a Pawn for nothing.

A configuration such as that in No. 113 (White Pawns at Q5, K4, Black at Q3, K4) where each Pawn is directly faced by one of the opposite color, is known as a *Pawn chain*. The Pawn which is farthest back (here Black's Pawn at Q3) is called the *base* of the chain. Such a chain cannot be weakened unless the base is removed. Therefore the theoretical plan for the superior side is *to attack the base of the Pawn chain.*

Applying this theory to No. 114, the indicated plan is an attack on Black's QBP. Thus: 1 P—QKt4! If then 1 .... P—QR3; 2 P—QR4, P—QKt3; 3 P×P, Q×P; 4 P—R5!, Q—Q1 (Note A.); 5 QR—Kt1 and the Black QBP is a backward Pawn on an open file. Note A. If 4 .... Q×KtP; 5 KR—Kt1 and the Q is lost. Or in the diagrammed position, 1 P—QKt4, P—QR3; 2 P—QR4, Kt—K1; 3 P—Kt5, RP×P; 4 P×P, R×R; 5 R×R, Kt—B2; 6 P—Kt6, Kt—K1; 7 R—R8 and Black is almost stalemated. Still another likelihood is 1 .... Kt—K1; 2 P—Kt5, Kt—B2; 3 QR—Kt1, P×P; 4 Kt×P, Kt×Kt; 5 R×Kt and Black besides being badly developed has a backward Pawn on an open file. The point is that no matter how Black plays, this attack against the base of the Pawn chain seriously weakens his Pawns and thereby yields White a concrete and permanent advantage.

Before leaving this section it is well to note one further point in attacks. In the above examples the center played no part in the proceedings. This was no accident, but was due to the fact that the attacker had neutralized the center before shifting to a wing. The principle is: Make sure that the center is solid before attacking on a wing. We shall see further justification for this in the discussion of the tenth rule.

V. EVEN POSITIONS

There are two questions that crop up when the game is even. First of all, how can I preserve equality? In other words, what problems will come up and how am I likely to go wrong? And secondly, how can I induce my opponent to weaken his position?

Neither of these questions can be answered in one sentence, except for that splendid bit of advice an elderly master once gave a promising young expert. The hopeful aspirant had come to his first international tournament and was scheduled to play one of the great stars in the first round. Chess players usually prefer to begin a strenuous contest by picking off a few easy marks. So our Young Hopeful was downcast and glum. Along comes the older expert and offers to give him a sure-fire method of beating his eminent opponent. Only to get the advice the young man would have to walk around the block with the older one six times. Eagerly the budding genius finished the required stretch, and then was rewarded with the sound counsel: "Always make the best move."

For those who find this a bit too general, we have to specify the answers to the two chief problems that come up—maintaining equilibrium, and creating weaknesses.

1. MAINTAINING EQUALITY

A complete discussion of this is really the task of half the book. Stick to all the positive rules; watch out for the pitfalls that have been noted. Remember, too, that every rule has its converse which tells you what not to do. E.g., since an attack must be conducted by opening a file (eighth rule) you should not create targets voluntarily. Do not move the Pawns near your King without good reason. Similarly, do not cramp your position, do not reduce the mobility of your pieces, etc. *Above all, do not weaken your Pawn position unnecessarily.* This is the most common reason why even games suddenly become inferior. Another is pointless exchanging, especially of an active piece for an inactive one.

Besides the long list of moves which are bad for reasons already mentioned, there is one positive general principle which is quite helpful in avoiding a bad game. That is the

NINTH RULE: CENTRALIZE THE ACTION OF ALL THE PIECES.

The center retains its importance throughout the game because it is the region of maximum mobility. Combinations are most effective when the pieces are in or near the center; attacks should not be begun unless control or neutralization of the center is assured. A better center is one form of positional advantage—try to prevent your opponent from securing one. Then too, by keeping your pieces trained on the center you can hardly drift into a cramped position because they all have maximum or near-maximum mobility.

2. CREATING WEAKNESSES

This is the converse of 1—how to induce your opponent to blunder. Assuming that the position is really even, a mistake is objectively the only winning chance. However, merely waiting for a mistake takes all the fun out of the game. The thing to do is to try to create positions where the best move is not so easy to find. Set problems for your opponent. In this way you will increase the likelihood of an inferior reply. No special principle can be used; every aspect of our general theory may be of use at one time or another in this connection.

A word must be said about traps. It is quite all right to set traps for the opponent, provided that declining the bait will not give him an immensely superior position. E.g., suppose that in the normal course of events you create a threat of winning his Queen. This is a trap in the strict sense, and there is nothing wrong with it. Presumably he will meet the threat and the game will go on. But suppose that you put a piece en prise to his Queen. If he does not see it he loses; if he does he captures your piece. Such a policy is short-sighted and quite bad. Or, to take a less drastic instance: we have often had occasion to refer to the trap that comes after 1 P—K4, P—K4; 2 B—B4, Kt—QB3; 3 Q—R5!? If Black does not notice the threat of Q×BP mate he loses at once, but if he does, and plays 3 .... P—KKt3, the White Queen must retreat with consequent loss of time. Such traps should be avoided. Now look at another case, a variation of the Queen's Gambit Declined. 1 P—Q4, P—Q4; 2 P—QB4, P—K3; 3 Kt—QB3, Kt—KB3; 4 B—Kt5, QKt—Q2! At first sight this looks dufferish, for 5 P×P, P×P; 6 Kt×P seems to win a Pawn. But the reply is 6 .... Kt×Kt; 7 B×Q, B—Kt5ch; 8 Q—Q2 (forced), B×Qch; 9 K×B, K×B and Black has won a piece. Such a trap, which arises in the normal course of development, is quite all right.

VI. INFERIOR POSITIONS

The art of defense is one of the most difficult on the chess board. For one thing, we all prefer to be aggressive, to have the upper hand, to dictate terms rather than to be pushed back, to be the underdog or to have to do what the other fellow tells us to. Then too, careful defense requires patience, calm, sometimes even in the face of insurmountable obstacles. Nevertheless, the ability to ward off an attack is just as vital and basic as the ability to launch one successfully.

The most important point about defensive tactics is psychological: never give up hope. Only too often even masters get into uncomfortable positions, become desperate, resort to some wild stab and resign before you can say P×P. Too many defenders are governed by the "Do or Die" philosophy, and usually die. What they forget is the old saw that "There's many a slip 'tween the cup and the lip." If a won game has been reached, it by no means follows that the opponent will play perfect chess and win it. Besides, there are many positions which look quite strong, which do in fact confer a real advantage, and which are still theoretically insufficient for a win. You must always take inferior moves and unforeseen possibilities into consideration and shape your plans accordingly—nobody ever plays perfectly or sees everything. The mistake, as Tartakover says somewhere, is the justification of chess. The thing to do is to maneuver in such a way that the opponent is more likely to go wrong than otherwise—to set difficult problems for him. Never forget that chess is a fight from start to finish.

Of course, we are talking about cases where there is still some real fight left. I.e., positions where one is one or two Pawns behind, or sometimes a piece for one Pawn, or where one has less mobility. If the material disadvantage is greater than a piece, the game can be saved only if the opponent makes an outright blunder.

When one is material behind, the best chance is an attack against the enemy King. For in such an attack the number of pieces in another part of the board is often irrelevant. This is still another aspect of our Principle of Safety. We can express this policy succinctly in our

TENTH RULE: THE BEST DEFENSE IS A COUNTER-ATTACK.

An excellent example of how such counterplay may become effective is seen in No. 115. There is no doubt that White has a winning advantage: he is a Pawn ahead and the Black King is exposed. Black must therefore pin all his hopes on a counter-attack. The game continued:

No. 115

18	P—K4
19 Kt—Kt3	Q—B4
20 Q—Q3	P—Q5!

Correctly assuming that the exchange of Queens is bad for White at the moment because it would stop the attack and saddle him with a weak QBP. E.g., 21 Q×Q, B×Q; 22 K—Q2, R—B1; 23 QR—B1, K—K2 and Black has good counter-chances.

Position after White's 18th move.

21 O—O	R—KKt1
22 P—KB4!	

White in his turn chooses to press the attack in order to exploit the exposed position of the Black King.

22	B—Kt2!

A pretty trap. If 23 Q×Q??, R×Pch; 24 K—R1, R—Kt6 dis ch; 25 R—B3, B×R mate.

23 R—B2	B—K5

Now he must finally attend to the Queen. Exchanging would be inferior because the Pawns are too weak for the ending: 23 .... Q×Q; 24 P×Q, K—K2; 25 R—K1, K—Q3; 26 P×Pch, P×P; 27 Kt—Q2, etc.

24 Q—Q2	K—B2!

Setting a new problem for White. On the obvious 25 P×P?, R×Pch!; 26 R×R, B×R gives Black a powerful attack.

25 R—K1	R—Kt5!

Again making it as hard as he can. White has a number of continuations to choose from, but only one is good: 26 P×P, Q×P; 27 P—KR3!, R—Kt3; 28 Q×P, with an easy win. He picks a move which looks equally good, but Black finds an ingenious resource.

26 Kt—B5?	B×KtP!!
27 R×B	QR—KKt1
28 R—K2	

If 28 R×R, Q×Rch leads to mate or the loss of White's Queen: 29 K—B1, Q—R6ch; 30 K—K2, R—Kt7ch; or 29 K—R1, Q—B6ch and mate next.

28	P×P!
29 Kt—Kt7	

Or 29 R×R, R×Rch and 30 .... Q×Kt.

29	Q—Q4
30 R×R	R×Rch
31 R—Kt2	R×Rch
32 Q×R	P—B6

and the game was ultimately drawn.

In defending when the disadvantage is positional, a counter-attack at all costs is not advisable, but one should always seek as much counterplay as possible. In accordance with our fourth rule, exchanges will free the game. Again, following the theory of Pawn play, Pawn moves near the King create targets and should be avoided. A good principle to adhere to in the defense of a King position is that one should react only to direct threats.

A splendid illustration of correct and careful defense against a King attack is No. 116 (from Alekhine [1]—Euwe,[2] Amsterdam, 1936). Black's position is cramped and White has a strong Pawn center. This does not mean that the second player is lost, so that desperate measures would be in order. But he will try to free his game. The game continued:

21	P—Q4!

First weakening the White Pawn center.

22 P—K5	Kt—R2
23 Kt—B5	P—B3

---

[1] Dr. Alexander Alekhine, 1892—, Franco-Russian star, is the present champion of the world.

[2] Dr. Max Euwe, 1901—, of Holland, captured the title from Alekhine in 1935, but lost the return match in 1937.

To get rid of the dangerous advanced Pawn.

No. 116

| 24 P—Kt4 | P×P |
| 25 B×KP | Kt—B3 |

Now Black has an exchange threat: 26 .... B—B2, for if in reply 27 Q×P, B×B equalizes. The Kt move made this possible by defending the Queen.

26 Q—Q3!

Position after White's 21st move.

So that if 26 .... B—B2?; 27 Kt×Pch, P×Kt; 28 Q—Kt6ch, Q—Kt2; 29 Q×Qch, K×Q; 30 B×B and White has won a Pawn.

| 26 .... | K—R1! |

With a view to the exchange plan.

27 R—KKt1	B—B2
28 P—B4	Q—B2
29 QR—KB1	

Black still has not freed his game effectively, but now aggressive counteraction does the trick.

29	B×B
30 BP×B	Kt—K5!
31 P—Kt5	

If 31 Kt×RP, Kt—B7ch; 32 K—Kt2, R×Kt; 33 R×Kt, R×Pch; 34 K×R, Q×Rch and Black cannot lose.

31	P×P
32 Kt—Q6	Kt—B7ch!
33 K—Kt2	Kt×Q
34 Kt×Qch	K—Kt1
35 Kt×P	R—Kt3

and Black has at least an even ending.

PROBLEMS

No. 25

White to play. What is his best plan and how should he work it out?

No. 26

White to play. What is a good plan?

No. 27

White to play. What should his plan be?

No. 28

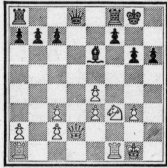

Who has the better Pawn position? What plans would you suggest for White and for Black?

No. 29

Who has the better game and why?

No. 30

White to play and win.

No. 31

White to play and win.

No. 32

White to play and win.

No. 33

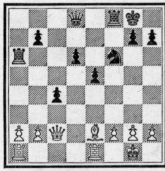

White to play and win.

No. 34

White to play and win.

No. 35

White to play and win.

No. 36

White to play and win.

No. 37

White to play and win.

No. 38

White to play and win.

No. 39

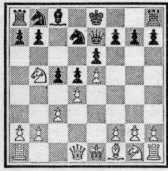

White to play and win.

No. 40

White to play and win.

No. 41

White to play and win.

No. 42

White to play and win.

No. 43

White to play and win.

No. 44

White to play and win.

No. 45

White to play and win.

No. 46

White to play and win.

No. 47

How should White continue the attack?

No. 48

Black has a cramped position. Can
you find a good defensive plan?

Chapter VII.

BASIC POSITIONS IN THE ENDGAME

The final part of the game is the one which is most subject to exact calculation. This is especially true when the amount of material has been reduced to only two or three units (not counting the Kings). In these latter cases the result can almost always be determined with mathematical certainty. For this reason, it is advisable to know the most important finales with a few men. Fortunately, the number of such positions is strictly limited. Since they are so fundamental we have included all in this chapter.

The most elementary type is that with nothing but Kings and Pawns —pure Pawn endings. King and Pawn vs. King is sometimes a win, sometimes a draw, but King and two Pawn vs. King is always a win.

Against one Pawn Black [1] has a chance only if his King can get in front of the Pawn and block it. An easy way to determine whether a King can catch a Pawn or not without actually counting the moves is the Rule of the Square (Diagram No. 117). Draw a square on the board, using the distance from the Pawn to the eighth rank as the side. (If the Pawn is on the second rank, begin the square from the third, because it can get to the fourth in one move.) Black's King must be inside the square, if it is White's turn, or one move away, if it is Black's turn, else the Pawn will queen unopposed. To be exact, we should draw two squares, one on each side of the Pawn, but the one on the left in No. 117 would consist of only two files. Besides, it would be quite obvious here that the Black King could play one file to the left and stop the Pawn.

Assuming then that the Black King is in the square of the Pawn, the critical position which determines the outcome is No. 118. Here it depends on whose move it is. Thus if Black plays, 1 .... K—K1 (Note A.); 2 P—K7 forces 2 .... K—B2, when 3 K—Q7, K—B3 (or anywhere else); 4 P—K8=Q wins. Note A. Or 1 .... K—B1; 2 P—K7 and promotes. But if White begins he cannot gain the

---

[1] It is convenient to speak of the materially inferior side as Black, and of the materially superior as White. This terminology will be used in this chapter and the next.

No. 117

In order to be able to catch the Pawn, Black's King must be inside the square, White to play, or be able to move into it, Black to play.

No. 118

Black to play loses; White to play draws.

necessary tempo: 1 P—K7ch, K—K1 and now 2 K—B6 loses the Pawn, while 2 K—K6 yields only the dubious satisfaction of stalemate.

In a position of the type of No. 118, if it is Black's move, White is said to have the *opposition*. The opposition is extremely valuable as a method of gaining control of squares in King and Pawn endings.

The general case with K+P vs. K is a draw if the White King is in back or to one side of the Pawn, but a win if it is in front of the Pawn. Nos. 119 and 120 illustrate the point.

In No. 119 Black draws by preventing the White King from getting in front of the Pawn and by retreating *straight back* whenever he is forced to give way. He must always retain the opposition. Thus:

No. 119

Draw.

No. 120

White wins.

1 .... K—K4; 2 P—K4, K—K3 (Note A.); 3 K—Q4, K—Q3; 4 P—
K5ch, K—K3; 5 K—K4, K—K2; 6 K—B5, K—B2! (Note B.); 7 P—
K6ch, K—K2; 8 K—K5, K—K1! (Note C.); 9 K—Q6, K—Q1 and
now we have the draw of No. 118, since White must move.

Note A. But not 2 .... K—B5??; 3 K—Q4 and Black will never
again be able to get back in front of the Pawn.

Note B. Not 6 .... K—Q2??; 7 K—B6, K—K1; 8 K—K6 and
wins because he has the opposition: 8 .... K—B1; 9 K—Q7, or 8 ....
K—Q1; 9 K—B7, followed by the advance of the Pawn in either case.

Note C. Again he has a chance to go wrong: 8 .... K—B1??;
9 K—B6, or 8 .... K—Q1??; 9 K—Q6, both transpose into the loss
of No. 118.

The advantage of having the King in front of the Pawn is seen in
No. 120. After 1 P—K4!, Black has to go to one side, when White
goes to the other and escorts the Pawn to the eighth: 1 P—K4, K—
B2; 2 K—Q6, K—K1; 3 K—K6, K—B1; 4 K—Q7, K—B2; 5 P—K5,
K—B1; 6 P—K6, K—Kt2; 7 P—K7, K—B2; 8 P—K8=Qch etc.
If Black had gone to the Q-file, White would have switched his King
to the B-file.

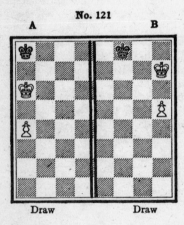

No. 121

A   B

Draw   Draw

A RP forms an exception to the
above rules because there is only
one side to go to. In No. 121A the
Black King can never be driven
out of the corner: he shunts his
King back and forth until peace
negotiations are completed: 1 P—
R5, K—Kt1; 2 K—Kt6 (too bad he
can't move off the board!), K—R1;
3 P—R6, K—Kt1; 4 P—R7ch,
K—R1; 5 K—R6, stalemate. In
No. 121B White either has to let
the Black King into the corner or
stalemate himself. Thus: 1 K—
Kt6, K—Kt1; 2 P—R6, K—R1 etc.
(No. 121A), or 1 P—R6, K—B2;
2 K—R8, K—B1; 3 P—R7, K—
B2, stalemate.

Other variants of this ending can be figured out by comparing them
with the basic positions given.

King and two Pawns always win vs. the lone King. We saw in
No. 118 that all that was needed for the win was one tempo. If there
is an extra Pawn, this problem is solved. The three possible cases are
shown in No. 122. In 122A straightforward pushing is enough, provided one is careful to avoid stalemate: 1 P—K4, K—Q3; 2 P—Q4,
K—B3; 3 K—B4, K—Q3; 4 P—K5ch, K—B3; 5 P—Q5ch, K—B2;

6 K—B5, K—Q2; 7 P—K6ch, K—B2; 8 P—Q6ch, K—Q1; 9 K—Kt6, K—B1; 10 P—Q7ch, K—Q1; 11 K—Kt7, K—K2; 12 K—B8 and queens.

Nos. 122B and C are somewhat different: here we advance one Pawn, keeping the other in the background to gain the needed tempo at the right time. Thus in 122B: 1 P—B4ch, K—B4; 2 K—B3, K—B3; 3 K—Q4, K—Q3; 4 P—B5ch, K—B3; 5 K—B4, K—B2; 6 K—Q5, K—Q2; 7 P—B6ch, K—B2; 8 K—B5, K—B1; 9 K—Q6, K—Q1; 10 P—B7ch, K—B1; 11 P—K4!, K—Kt2; 12 K—Q7 and

No. 122A

White wins.

No. 122B

White wins.

promotes. The same sort of thing holds for No. 122C. This last is the most dangerous case: if both Pawns are advanced too hastily the game may well be drawn.

Since two Pawns win, a greater number of Pawns will, of course, also succeed. Always try to force a Queen at the earliest possible moment and watch out for stalemate!

A minor piece (Bishop or Knight) is equivalent to three Pawns in the ending. However, the placement of the Pawns may alter matters, for two Pawns on the seventh are far better than a piece.

No. 122C

White wins.

Bishop or Knight vs. one Pawn is always a draw because the piece can be sacrificed for the Pawn if the worst comes to the worst.

Two passed Pawns vs. a lone minor piece offer winning chances chiefly when they are connected. In that event, if the enemy King is nearby they draw, but if he is far away they win. The two possibilities are seen in No. 123. In 123A after 1 .... K—Kt7; 2 P—B5, K—B6; 3 P—B6, B—Kt6; 4 P—Kt5, B—B2; 5 K—B5, K—Q5; 6 P—Kt6, B—R7; 7 P—B7 White queens. But in 123B on 1 P—B5, K—B2; 2 P—Kt5, even 2 .... B×P! draws (No. 119).

Three Pawns present a more complicated picture. If they are far apart they will win, regardless of the position of the Black King. Thus in No. 124 White wins because the Black King has to make up his mind. If he sticks to the two Pawns, they will support one another, and enable their own King to go to the Q-side and pick up the B there. If he switches over to the one Pawn, the two Pawns will march on. E.g., 1 .... K—B3; 2 K—B6, B—K6; 3 P—B5, K—Kt4; 4 P—R5, K—B3 (Note A.); 5 P—R6, K—Kt4; 6 K—Kt7, K—B3; 7 P—R7, B×P; 8 K×B followed by going back to the other wing. Note A. If 4 .... K×P; 5 P—B6, K—B4; 6 P—B7, B—R3; 7 P—R6 and one of the Pawns will queen. Another possibility from the original position is 1 .... K—Q2; 2 P—B5, B—K6; 3 P—R5, K—B2; 4 P—R6, K—Kt3; 5 P—B6, K×P; 6 P—B7, B—R3; 7 P—Kt5, B—B1; 8 K—K6, K—Kt2; 9 K—Q7, K—Kt3; 10 K—K8, B—Kt2; 11 P—B8=Q, B×Q; 12 K×B etc.

However, three connected passed Pawns win only if they are all beyond the fourth rank and are not blockaded. Four Pawns will always win.

A minor piece plus a Pawn will always win against the lone King, except for one special case. In No. 125 the win is again made possible by the extra tempo which the piece confers. 1 P—K4ch, K—K3; 2 K—Q4, K—Q3; 3 B—Kt4ch, K—K3; 4 P—K5, K—Q2; 5 K—Q5, K—Q1; 6 P—K6, K—K1; 7 K—Q6, K—Q1; 8 P—K7ch, K—K1;

No. 123A   No. 123B

White wins.   Draw.

No. 124

White wins.

No. 125

White wins.

No. 126

Draw. Win with Bishop on Black squares.

No. 127

White wins.

9 B—Q2, K—B2; 10 K—Q7, etc.

The exception occurs with a RP plus a Bishop which does not cover the queening square. This is known as RP+B of the wrong color (No. 126). The trouble is that the King cannot be driven out of the corner. 1 K—Kt5, K—R1; 2 K—R6, K—Kt1; 3 B—B4ch, K—R1! and 4 P—R5 stalemates. Nothing can ever happen to Black if he keeps on moving in and out of his hiding place. A Bishop of the other color in No. 126 would decide quite easily. E.g., place the B at K3 instead of Q3. Then 1 K—Kt5, K—R2; 2 P—R5, K—Kt2; 3 P—R6ch, K—R2; 4 K—R5, K—R1; 5 K—Kt6, K—Kt1; 6 B—Q4 compels 6 .... K—B1, when 7 P—R7 is conclusive.

A draw with Kt+P vs. K occurs in only a few problem cases.

When the White King is not in the neighborhood, the Pawn must be held by the minor piece until the King can approach. A Bishop can defend a P from any position, but a Knight must be behind it. E.g., if the Pawn is at Q3, the B may be anywhere on a diagonal to defend the Pawn. But the Kt must be at K1, B1, QKt2 or KB2, for if the Black King then attacks both Kt and P, it will never be able to capture the Kt without leaving the square of the Pawn. Again, if the Kt were at K5, P at Q3, Black could play .... K—Q5 and could take the Kt and still stop the Pawn.

When White is a piece ahead, and both sides have Pawns, three Pawns for the piece draw, two lose, four or more win. The typical win against two Pawns is shown in No. 127. The idea is to penetrate to the Pawns with the King and capture more material. As soon as an opportunity is seen to force a passed Pawn and advance it, it should be grasped. A likely continuation is 1 .... K—B2; 2 K—B2, K—K3; 3 K—K3, K—Q4; 4 K—B4, K—K3; 5 K—K4, P—KKt3; 6 B—B3, P—B4ch; 7 P×Pch, P×Pch; 8 K—B4, P—Kt4; 9 P—R5, P—QR3; 10 P—QR3, K—Q4; 11 K×P, K—B5; 12 B—Kt4, K—Kt6; 13 K—B6, K—R5; 14 K—Kt7, P—R4; 15 B—Q6, P—Kt5; 16 P×P, P×P; 17 K×P, P—Kt6; 18 B—K5, K—R6; 19 K—Kt7, P—Kt7; 20 B×Pch, K×B; 21 P—R6 and the rest is simple. Note that White proceeds by first fixing a Pawn on a certain square (here the Black KBP), then attacking it with the King, and finally forcing the Black King to abandon it.

The danger in this and similar instances is that too many Pawns will be exchanged. E.g., in No. 127, if we remove the Black QRP and QKtP, White QRP and KKtP, then .... P—KR4 followed by .... P—KKt4 will get rid of the last Pawn and automatically draw.

A piece plus Pawn vs. a piece is a draw if the enemy King is in front of the Pawn, but a win if he is far away. In No. 128 Black merely moves his Knight back and forth—his King can only be budged by a

No. 128   No. 129

Draw.   White wins.

No. 130A

White wins.

No. 130B

White wins.

No. 130C

Draw.

No. 131

White wins.

ton of nitroglycerine, a commodity ordinarily not available near the chess table.   But in No. 129 the Black Knight can be prevented from sacrificing itself for the Pawn: 1 .... K—Kt7; 2 P—B6, Kt—R2; 3 P—B7, K—B6; 4 B—Q4, Kt—B1; 5 B—B5, K—B5; 6 K—B6, K—K4; 7 K—Q7, K—Q4; 8 K×Kt, etc.   With Kt+P vs. B there are a few drawn cases.

A piece plus two Pawns vs. a piece is always a win, unless the Pawns are doubled or blockaded.   The idea is to capture the enemy man for one Pawn, when you are left with piece plus Pawn vs. the lone King.

The case where the two Pawns are connected is seen in No. 130A. Here the win requires nothing more than a judicious advance of the Pawns.   Avoid a blockade by always keeping at least one Pawn on the color opposite to that of the Bishop (thus here on White).   The model procedure is: 1 P—B5ch, K—Q3; 2 K—B4, K—K2; 3 P—K5, K—K1; 4 P—K6, Kt—B1; 5 B—B5, Kt—R2; 6 K—K5, Kt—Kt4; 7 P—B6, Kt—B6ch; 8 K—B4, Kt—R5; 9 P—B7ch, K—Q1; 10 P—B8=Qch.

In No. 130B the procedure is somewhat different. Here the Black Bishop is compelled to keep an eye on one Pawn and the King on the other. Consequently White can win a piece by concentrating on the Bishop: 1 .... K—B2; 2 P—QKt6, B—B1; 3 Kt—Kt5, K—Kt3; 4 K—B4, K—Kt2; 5 Kt—Q6, B—R3; 6 P—Kt7, etc. Another successful stratagem here would be to win the Bishop with the King and hold the Pawn with the Kt: 1 .... K—B2; 2 P—QKt6, B—B1; 3 K—Q6, K—Kt3; 4 K—B7, B—R3; 5 Kt—B3, K—B4; 6 P—Kt7, B×P; 7 K×B, K—Kt3; 8 K—B6, K—B4; 9 K—Q5, K—Kt3; 10 K—K4, K—B2; 11 K—B5, etc.

The danger in these endings is exemplified in No. 130C, where the Pawns are blockaded. No powers of chessic persuasion can induce the Black monarch to desert his impregnable fortress, and the nimble horseman can ride about indefinitely. 1 K—B4, Kt—Q2; 2 B—R4, Kt—K4; 3 B—Kt5, Kt—B2, etc.—the Kt can never be stalemated and will always have the square K4 covered. This type of blockade is most effectively carried out by a Kt, although there are positions where a B is just as good.

With three Pawns the blockade can never work. In No. 131, after 1 .... Kt—Q2; 2 K—Q4, Kt—K4; 3 P—Q6, Kt—Q2; 4 B—R4, Kt—K4; 5 K—Q5 Black can no longer hold up the enemy infantry: 5 .... Kt—B6; 6 P—Q7, K—K2; 7 P—B6ch, K—Q1; 8 P—B7, K—K2; 9 P—B8=Qch, K×Q; 10 P—Q8=Qch and wins.

An exception to the rule that unblocked Pawns win occurs with Bishops of opposite colors. Here connected Pawns only draw (unless they are on the sixth or beyond), while disconnected ones win.

In No. 132A Black keeps his Bishop on the long diagonal and White will never be able to break through, for P—Q5ch at any time is cracked by .... B×P. Nor is 1 K—K3, B—R1; 2 K—Q3, B—Kt2; 3 B—R3, B—R1, etc., of any use. But No. 132B is won because the two Black pieces cannot cooperate—one must hold one Pawn, while the other guards the other: 1 P—QKt5, K—Q4; 2 P—Kt5, K—K3; 3 P—KKt6, K—K2; 4 P—Kt7, K—B2; 5 K—B4, K—Kt1; 6 K—B5, K—B2; 7 K—Kt6, B—Kt7; 8 K—B7, K—Kt1; 9 P—Kt6, K—B2; 10 P—Kt7, B×P; 11 K×B, K—Kt1; 12 K—B6, K—B2; 13 K—Q5, K—Kt1; 14 K—K6, K—R2; 15 K—B7, etc.

If the Pawns are on the sixth in No. 132A they will always win because Black has too little leeway for his pieces. Thus in No. 132C, 1 K—Kt6 is conclusive, for if 1 .... K—B1; 2 P—K7. On 1 .... B—Kt4; 2 K—B7 or 2 K×B are both good enough. However, if the Pawns are blockaded, i.e., all on the same color as the Bishop, they

No. 132A

Draw.

No. 132B

White wins.

will never win: the situation would be essentially the same as that in No. 130C.

Three Pawns always win, but even here one should be careful not to blockade the Pawns. Remember that a cardinal principle in all phases of the game is that one must keep the Pawns mobile.

Rook endings obey different laws because a Rook is enough to mate with. With a Rook vs. Pawns, if all the Pawns are captured, the Rook will therefore win.

No. 132C

White wins.

No. 133

Draw.

No. 134A

White wins.

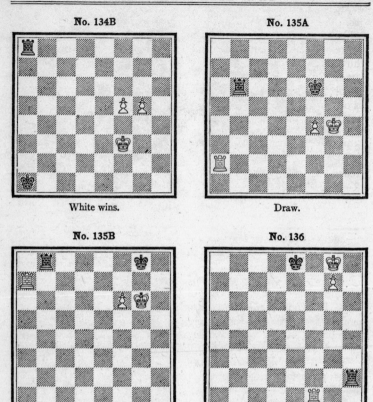

No. 134B

White wins.

No. 135A

Draw.

No. 135B

White wins.

No. 136

White wins.

Rook vs. one Pawn wins if the White King is near the scene of
action, but only draws if it is far away. Thus in No. 133, after 1 K—
B6, P—Kt6; 2 R—KKt8, K—B6; 3 K—Q5, P—Kt7; 4 K—Q4, K—
B7; 5 R—B8ch, K—K7; 6 R—KKt8, K—B7 White can at best give
up his Rook for the strong enemy passed Pawn. But if the White
King were at KKt2 in No. 133 the win would be child's play. The
Pawn would be captured in short order.

Against two Pawns the Rook again wins if the King is in the
neighborhood. The idea in No. 134A is to blockade and then capture
the luckless soldiers: 1 .... K—B4; 2 K—B2, K—Kt4; 3 K—K3,
P—R6; 4 K—B2, K—R5; 5 R—Kt4!, K—Kt4; 6 K—Kt3, K—B4;
7 R×P, P—R7; 8 R—KR4 etc. However, if the King is not in the
neighborhood, two connected passed Pawns cannot be held by a
Rook. E.g., in No. 134B: 1 .... K—Kt7; 2 P—Kt6, K—B6; 3 P—

Kt7, K—Q5; 4 P—B6, K—K4; 5 P—B7, K—B3; 6 P—B8 = Qch and wins. This is only true of connected passed Pawns: disconnected and doubled Pawns can at best only draw.

Three Pawns, if connected and far advanced, will draw even if White's King is in front of them. Four Pawns will always at least draw, while they may frequently win.

Rook and Pawns vs. Pawns is a win in practically all cases, regardless of the number of Pawns for the Rook, because the side with the Rook can set up a passed Pawn and queen it.

Rook and Pawn vs. Rook is a draw if the Black King is in front of the Pawn, but a win if it is not. The general draw, as in No. 135A, is achieved by keeping the Rook on the third rank until the Pawn reaches the sixth, and then playing to the eighth: 1 .... K—Kt3; 2 R—R2, K—Kt2; 3 K—Kt5, R—QR3; 4 P—B5, R—QKt3; 5 R—

No. 137

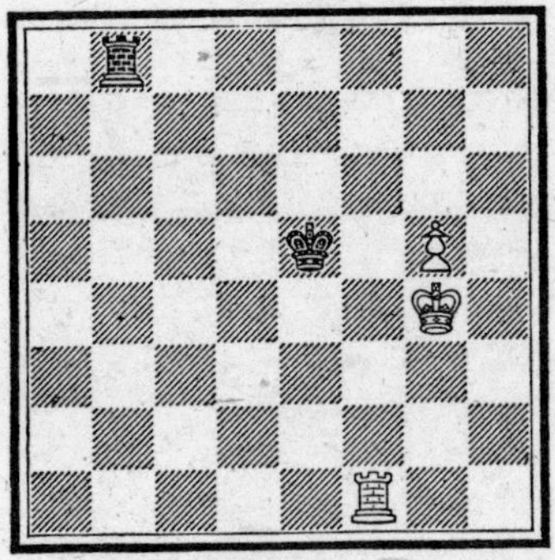

White wins.

No. 138

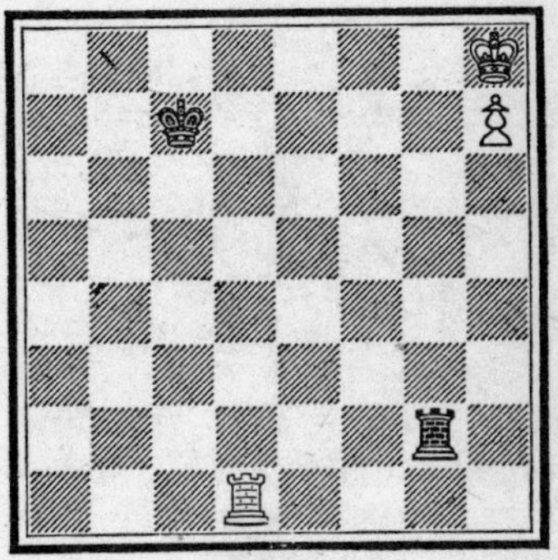

White wins.

No. 139A

White wins.

No. 139B

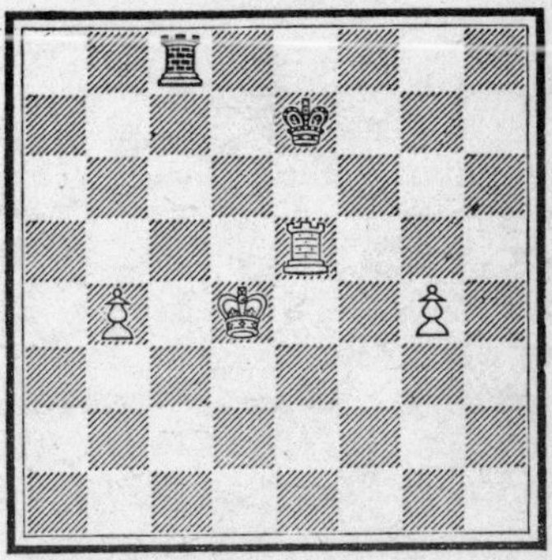

White wins.

No. 139C

Draw.

No. 140

White wins.

R2, R—QB3; 6 R—R7ch, K—Kt1; 7 P—B6, R—B8! (for what happens if this is not played, see No. 135B); 8 K—Kt6, R—Kt8ch; 9 K—B5, K—B1; 10 K—K6, R—K8ch; 11 K—B5, K—Kt1; 12 R—R8ch, K—B2 etc.—the Pawn has been stopped. But if Black has played weakly and allowed himself to be driven back, he gets to No. 135B, where White wins in a walk: 1 .... R—Q1; 2 R—Kt7ch, K—B1; 3 R—KR7, K—Kt1; 4 P—B7ch, K—B1; 5 R—R8ch, K—K2; 6 R×R, K×R; 7 P—B8=Qch etc.

With the Black King cut off from the Pawn, White wins. The key position is No. 136. It will not do to get the King out at once by 1 R—K1ch, K—Q2; 2 K—B7 because 2 .... R—B7ch will eventually force him back to the same place. Still, White can get his King out favorably by placing the Rook on the fourth rank: 1 .... K—K2; 2 R—B4, R—R8; 3 R—K4ch, K—Q3 (Note A.); 4 K—B7, R—B8ch; 5 K—Kt6, R—Kt8ch; 6 K—B6, R—B8ch; 7 K—Kt5, R—Kt8ch; 8 R—Kt4 and wins.

Note A. If 3 .... K—B3; 4 K—B8, R—R8; 5 P—Kt8=Q, R—R1ch; 6 R—K8 etc.

If the Pawn has not yet reached the seventh, it is essential to get it at least to the fifth as soon as possible. From No. 137 we proceed as follows: 1 .... R—Kt1; 2 K—R5, R—R1ch; 3 K—Kt6, R—Kt1ch; 4 K—R6, R—R1ch; 5 K—Kt7, R—R7; 6 P—Kt6, R—KKt7; 7 K—R7, R—R7ch; 8 K—Kt8, K—K3; 9 P—Kt7, K—K2; 10 R—B4 etc. as in No. 136.

A RP is an exception to the usual rules. Here the enemy King must be at least four files away (on the QB file with a KRP, on the KB file with a QRP) if White is to be able to win. In No. 138 the procedure has some tricky points: 1 R—QR1, K—Q2; 2 R—R8, K—K3; 3 R—KKt8, R—QR7; 4 K—Kt7, R—Kt7ch; 5 K—B8, R—B7ch; 6 K—

K8, R—QR7; 7 R—Kt6ch, K—B4; 8 R—B6ch!!, K×R; 9 P—R8=
Qch, etc.—Queen vs. Rook is a theoretical win.

Rook and two Pawns vs. Rook is always a win, with the usual
exceptions of doubled and blockaded Pawns.

With connected Pawns, the greatest practical difficulties come up in
No. 139A. One must always take care to have a flight square for the
King (where no check is possible) and to avoid a blockade of the
Pawns. The model win is 1 R—K5! (Note A.), R—R6; 2 P—R4,
R—QKt6; 3 P—R5ch, K—R3; 4 R—KB5, R—QR6; 5 R—B3, R—
R8; 6 K—Kt3, R—Kt8ch; 7 K—R4, R—R8ch; 8 R—R3, R—KKt8;
9 R—R2! (Note B.), R—QR8; 10 P—Kt5ch, K—Kt2; 11 R—KB2,
R—R8ch; 12 K—Kt4, R—Kt8ch; 13 K—B5, R—KR8; 14 P—R6ch,
K—R2; 15 R—B4, R—KKt8; 16 R—K4, R—B8ch; 17 K—Kt4, R—
Kt8ch; 18 K—R5, R—R8ch; 19 R—R4, R—KKt8; 20 R—R2, R—
Kt6; 21 R—K2, R—R6ch; 22 K—Kt4, R—R6; 23 R—K7ch, K—
Kt1; 24 P—Kt6, R—R5ch; 25 K—B5, R—R4ch; 26 R—K5, R—R1;
27 K—B6, R—R3ch; 28 R—K6, R—R1; 29 R—Q6, R—K1; 30 R—
Q5, R—R1; 31 K—K7, R—R2ch; 32 R—Q7, R—R1; 33 R—Q8ch
and wins.

Note A. Essential to defend the King from checks. If 1 P—R4?,
R—B7ch; 2 K—B3, R—B6ch; 3 K—B4, R—B5ch; 4 K—B3, R—
B6ch; 5 K—Kt2, R—B7ch; 6 K—Kt1, R—B5 and will draw.

Note B. One of the Black pieces must now give way. Such a
position, where there is no direct threat but any move made is harmful, is known as *zugzwang* (literally move forced).

With disconnected Pawns the idea is to use one Pawn to deflect the
King, and to win with the other. Thus in No. 139B White will merely
stay on the side opposite the Black King, giving up one Pawn to
force an easy win with R+P vs. K: 1 .... K—B3; 2 P—QKt5, R—
B8; 3 R—K2, K—Kt4; 4 P—Kt6, K×P; 5 K—Q5, K—B6; 6 R—K8,
R—QKt8; 7 K—B6, R—B8ch; 8 K—Q7, R—QKt8; 9 K—B7, R—
B8ch; 10 K—Kt8, R—QKt8; 11 P—Kt7, K—B5; 12 K—R7, R—
R8ch; 13 K—Kt6, R—Kt8ch; 14 K—B6, R—B8ch; 15 K—Q5 and
after the checks are exhausted Black will also be all worn out and will
have to give up his Rook for the Pawn.

The danger is as usual the blockade. In No. 139C the Black King
cannot be driven away from QB5 without sacrificing a Pawn, which
is not good enough: 1 R—R8, K×P; 2 P—Kt5, R—QKt8; 3 R—
QKt8, K—B5; 4 P—Kt6, K—Kt4; 5 K—Q6, K—R3; 6 K—B7,
R—B8ch; 7 K—Q7, R—B7 and draws.

With three Pawns a blockade can always be broken. E.g., in No.
140: 1 R—K3, R—Q7; 2 K—Q6, R—KR7; 3 P—Q5, R—R3ch;
4 R—K6, R—R6; 5 K—B6, R×P; 6 P—Q6, K×P dis ch; 7 K—Kt7,
R—Q6; 8 K—B7, R—B6ch; 9 K—Q8, R—Q6; 10 P—Q7, K—B4;
11 K—K8 and Black's Rook will soon go.

In Queen and Pawn endings two new elements come in—the power
of the Queen and the danger of perpetual check. These factors lead
to two curious results—a Queen can win against any number of Pawns,
and only Q+3P vs. Q win with ease.

With a Queen vs. Pawns, the little fellows usually give up the ghost
as soon as they see the big woman. So many check-and-capture combinations are possible that a Queen wins against any number of Pawns
in almost any position (unless two or more are on the seventh rank).
The general win with Q vs. P is shown in No. 141A. The idea is to
force the Black King in front of his Pawn, thus gaining time for White
to bring his King up: 1 Q—Q5ch, K—B7; 2 Q—K4ch, K—Q7; 3 Q—
Q4ch, K—B7; 4 Q—K3! (the key move), K—Q8; 5 Q—Q3ch, K—K8;
6 K—Kt5, K—B7; 7 Q—B5ch, K—Kt7; 8 Q—K4ch, K—B7; 9 Q—
B4ch, K—Kt7; 10 Q—K3!, K—B8; 11 Q—B3ch, K—K8; 12 K—B4,

No. 141A

White to play wins.

No. 141B

No. 141B

Draw.

No. 141C

Draw.

No. 141D

White to play wins.

No. 142   No. 143

Draw.   White wins.

K—Q7; 13 Q—K3ch, K—Q8; 14 Q—Q3ch, K—K8; 15 K—B3, K—B8; 16 Q×Pch, K—Kt8; 17 Q—Kt2 mate.

Stalemate possibilities make the BP and RP exceptions. Thus in No. 141B, after 1 Q—Q4ch, K—R7; 2 Q—B3, K—Kt8; 3 Q—Kt3ch, K—R8! saves Black, since 4 Q×P is stalemate. Similarly, in No. 141C, on 1 Q—Kt4ch, K—R8! the stalemate threat prevents White from bringing his King up. However, if either BP or RP is on the sixth, the Queen will mop up.

An important exception to the exceptions is No. 141D where White gleefully permits Black to queen and then mates him: 1 Q—Q2ch, K—Kt8; 2 K—Kt4, P—R8=Q; 3 K—Kt3!!, Q—K4; 4 Q—Q1 mate.

Queen and Pawn vs. Queen is as a rule only drawn because the White King cannot escape perpetual check. White can win only in certain positions with a center Pawn or BP on the seventh. The type draw with a KtP is shown in No. 142. Black can even allow White to queen: 1 .... Q—K1ch!; 2 P—Kt8=Q, Q—K4ch; 3 Q(R7)—Kt7, Q—R4ch; 4 Q(Kt8)—R7, Q—K1ch; 5 Q(Kt7)—Kt8, Q—K4ch etc., and both sides will soon stop playing ring-around-the-rosy.

The winning stratagem in such endings is to avoid perpetual check by threatening to interpose with check. A vital case where this can be done with two Pawns is No. 143. After 1 .... Q—K1ch; 2 K—B4, Q—K7ch; 3 K—B5, Q—K2ch; 4 Q—Q6, Q—Kt4ch; 5 K—B6, Q—Kt7ch; 6 K—B7, Q—Kt2ch; 7 Q—Q7 Black has run out of good checks because White can discover check. The end might be 7 .... Q—B6ch; 8 K—Q6 dis ch, K—Kt1; 9 Q—Kt5ch, K—B1; 10 Q—B6ch, exchanging Queens.

Still, there are many cases where two Pawns are not enough to safeguard the King from perpetual check. A certain win occurs only with Q+3P vs. Q. The idea is then to advance the Pawns until one queens, meanwhile taking care to keep the King away from too many checks.

Without Pawns, a Queen alone always wins against a single unit, but can only draw against Rook plus piece, or three minor pieces.

The mate with Q vs. Kt (No. 144) is straightforward. 1 .... Kt—K3; 2 K—Q5, Kt—B2ch; 3 K—K5, Kt—K1; 4 Q—K6ch, K—Q1; 5 Q—B7, Kt—B2; 6 K—Q6, Kt—Kt4ch; 7 K—B5, Kt—B2; 8 K—B6, Kt—R3; 9 Q—Q7 mate.

No. 144	No. 145
White wins.	White wins.

Q vs. R is more difficult. The idea is to force Black into a position where King and Rook must part, when a check will pick up the Rook. From No. 145 best play is 1 Q—R8ch! (Note A.), K—B2; 2 Q—R7ch, K—K1; 3 Q—Kt8ch, K—K2; 4 Q—QB8, R—Q7; 5 Q—B5ch, K—Q2; 6 Q—Kt5ch, K—B1; 7 K—K6, R—QB7; 8 K—Q6, R—KR7; 9 Q—K8ch, K—Kt2; 10 Q—K4ch, K—Kt3; 11 Q—KB4, R—R4; 12 Q—K3ch, K—R4; 13 K—B6, K—Kt5; 14 Q—Q4ch, K—R4; 15 Q—Q2ch, K—R5; 16 Q—Q1ch and 17 Q×R.

Note A. There are numerous stalemate traps for the unwary. If e.g., 1 K—K6??, R—Q3ch!!! forces 2 K×R, stalemate.

Queen vs. Rook and piece is only drawn.

Summary: With an advantage of one Pawn, the game is always drawn if the Black King gets in front of the Pawn, but otherwise won with anything but Bishops of opposite colors or Queens. Two Pawns ahead will win unless they are doubled or blockaded. The usual winning idea with connected passed Pawns is to advance them side by side until they force the sacrifice of the last enemy unit. With disconnected Pawns, however, one is pushed through to the eighth, while the other is held in reserve. The one that is not held by the enemy King is to be advanced. Bishops of opposite colors almost always draw with two connected passed Pawns, while Queen endings are frequently drawn even when White is two Pawns to the good. An advantage of three Pawns or a piece (with Pawns on the board) is always sufficient for a win. The easiest endings to bring to a successful conclusion are those with only Pawns on the board.

PROBLEMS

No. 49

No. 50

Black to play and draw.

White to play and win.

No. 51

No. 52

White to play and win.

White to play and win.

No. 53

White to play. What should the result be?

No. 54

White to play and win.

No. 55

White to play and win.

No. 56

White to play and win.

No. 57

White to play and win.

No. 58

White to play and win.

No. 59

No. 60

White to play and win. What happens
if Black moves?

White to play and win.

Chapter VIII

TEN RULES FOR THE ENDING

The dividing line between middle game and ending is rather difficult to draw. Nevertheless, the characteristic feature of an endgame, as distinct from other phases, is quite clear: it is greater King activity. For once the number of pieces has been substantially reduced there is little or no danger of a mating attack. We may set up a convenient rule-of-thumb that the ending has been reached when there are not more than four pieces on each side, without Queens, or three pieces with Queens.

The finale should be the easiest part of the game, yet even to experienced players it is sometimes a medley of unsolvable mysteries. However, the leading ideas are both few in number and easily grasped, so that the reader will be able to secure a firm foundation for practical play from this chapter.

While almost all endings involve Pawns, some occasionally come up which do not. For these we have our

FIRST RULE: TO WIN WITHOUT PAWNS YOU MUST BE AT LEAST A ROOK OR TWO PIECES AHEAD.

If you are a Rook ahead, say R+B vs. B the mate proceeds in much the same manner as the simpler case with the Rook alone—drive the King back to the edge of the board, avoid stalemate.

Endings with Rook vs. Bishop and Rook vs. Knight are drawn, but in each there is a characteristic trap. With R vs. B Black must head for the corner which is not of the same color as the Bishop. Thus in No. 146A, after 1 R—Kt8ch, B—Kt1; 2 R—R8 would be stalemate, while 2 K—Kt5, K—Kt2 is meaningless. But if Black goes to the wrong corner, as in No. 146B, he loses: 1 .... B—B2; 2 R—KB6, B—Kt1; 3 R—B8, B—K3; 4 R—B1, B—B5; 5 R—R1ch, B—R3 and now the tempo move 6 R—R2! wins the B and mates.

With a Kt, Black should stay in the center of the board because a Kt in the corner has so few moves. The difference is seen in the two halves of No. 147. In A, 1 R—B7ch, K—Kt1; 2 R—B3, Kt—K3;

No. 146A

Draw.

No. 146B

White wins.

No. 147A

Draw.

No. 147B

White wins.

3 R—K3, Kt—Q1; 4 R—K8, K—B1 leads to nothing. But in 147B, on 1 R—K7, K—B1 allows 2 R—K8 mate, while on other moves the Kt is captured.

In the usual case, where both sides have Pawns, the basic new element which the ending introduces is the

SECOND RULE: THE KING MUST BE ACTIVE IN THE END-GAME.

This does not contradict the Principle of Safety because once the number of pieces is greatly reduced (especially with the Queens gone) mate dangers evaporate. However, check-capture combinations may turn up at any time.

Just where the King should be depends on the position. If there are passed Pawns it should support them; if there are weak enemy

Pawns it should try to attack them. A good policy to follow is that
as soon as the endgame starts the King should be brought near the
center.

We have repeatedly emphasized the point that with a material advantage one should exchange and head for the ending. The chief
reason for this is that the best counterchance—an attack against the
King—automatically has the sting taken out of it.

Now we must consider the technique of winning a won endgame.

If you are more than a piece ahead, and have a passed Pawn, advance it until the enemy has to give up another piece for it. Then,
with two pieces to the good, you can either capture more Pawns or
play directly for mate. If you have no passed Pawn, try to set one
up. Remember that with a piece to the good you can always capture
Pawns by first exposing them and then concentrating superior forces
on that point. But in all cases the winning procedure revolves about
the passed Pawn, and the method of exploiting it is the

THIRD RULE: PASSED PAWNS MUST BE PUSHED.

The effectiveness of this rule in bringing about a quick conclusion

No. 148

No. 149

White wins.   White wins.

may be seen from No. 148. Although White is a Rook ahead, the
game might drag on for a long time if he played weakly. But 1 P—R5!
decides quickly: 1 .... R—R1; 2 P—R6, R—R2. Now that the Pawn
is stopped (the stopping piece is called a *blockader*) the thing to do is
to remove the blockader in order to free the road for the Pawn. Thus:
3 R(B1)—Kt1, Kt—K5; 4 R—Kt7, R—R1; 5 P—R7, K—R2; 6 R—
Kt8 and wins a Rook for the Pawn, after which the rest is a simple
mopping-up operation: 6 .... R×P; 7 R×R, K—Kt3; 8 B—Q3,
P—B4; 9 B×Kt, QP×B; 10 R(Kt8)—Kt7, K—B3; 11 R×P, K—K4;

12 R—Kt6, K—Q4; 13 R×RP. Now White may either continue his meal and finish off the other Pawns, or advance his own RP, queen it, and then mate.

As a rule, it is rather difficult to go out directly for mate when there is no Queen. This is why the simplest method of winning is getting a passed Pawn and queening it.

Where there is no passed Pawn, the extra piece should be used to capture material and create one. Thus in No. 149 White must get his pieces into the Black position. This he can do by seizing the open file. 1 R(B1)—B1, R(B1)—B1; 2 B—K2! (to drive the Black Rook away), K—B1; 3 B—R6, R×R; 4 R×R, R—Q1; 5 R—B7, Kt—K1; 6 R×Pch, K—Kt1; 7 R×RP, Kt—Q3; 8 R—Q7, R×R; 9 Kt×R, P—QKt4; 10 Kt—B5, K—B2; 11 Kt—Kt7 and Black must exchange or give up another Pawn. In either event, White will set up a passed Pawn on the Q-side and advance it until he captures more material or queens. E.g., 11 .... Kt×Kt; 12 B×Kt, K—K2; 13 K—B1, K—Q3; 14 B—R6, K—B3; 15 K—K2, P—Kt5; 16 K—Q3, K—Q3; 17 K—B2, K—B3; 18 K—Kt3, K—Kt3; 19 B—Q3, P—R3; 20 K×P, K—B3; 21 P—QR4, K—Kt3; 22 P—R5ch, K—B3; 23 K—R4 etc. Note that once his last piece is gone Black is reduced to pure passivity. This is why the defender can often be compelled to weaken his position considerably by the necessity for avoiding an exchange.

Endings where one is a piece or more to the good are so simple that a little practice is enough to make you perfect in them.

With two Pawns ahead, the case is usually a bit more difficult. However, the third rule still holds and, if applied judiciously, will soon net the gain of a piece. Our middle game rule that the side who has more material should exchange is likewise quite useful. As a matter of fact, a won game becomes progressively easier to win as the number of pieces diminishes. This is expressed in the

FOURTH RULE: THE EASIEST ENDINGS TO WIN ARE PURE PAWN ENDINGS.

No. 150 illustrates the ease with which such a pure Pawn ending can be conducted to a successful conclusion. In No. 150A, the two Pawns are connected, so that they may be advanced without any danger, provided they are kept not more than one rank apart. Thus: 1 P—QR4, K—K2; 2 P—R5, K—Q2; 3 P—QKt4 (Note A.), K—B3; 4 P—R6, K—Kt3; 5 P—Kt5! This is the typical position where two connected passed Pawns defend one another. If 5 .... K×P; 6 P—R7 forces a Queen. As a result Black must mark time with his King and give White a chance to come up. With the Pawn position symmetrical on the K-side, as in No. 150A, no passed Pawn can be forced. This is an important point to bear in mind, for if the defender can create a passed Pawn, it must be taken care of before one can become aggressive. After 5 P—Kt5, the most likely continuation is 5 .... K—R2; 6 K—B1, K—Kt3; 7 K—K2, K—R2; 8 K—Q3, K—Kt3; 9 K—B3, K—R2; 10 K—Kt4, K—Kt3; 11 K—R4, P—B3; 12 K—Kt4, P—K4; 13 P—B4, P—K5; 14 P—B5, K—R2; 15 K—R5, K—Kt1; 16 P—Kt6, K—R1; 17 K—Kt5, K—Kt1; 18 K—B6, K—R1; 19 K—B7, P—R4; 20 P—Kt7ch, K—R2; 21 P—Kt8=Qch, K×P; 22 Q—Kt6 mate.

Note A. 3 P—R6, K—B3; 4 P—R7??, K—Kt2 costs White a Pawn.

If the Pawns are disconnected, as in No. 150B, they must not go forward indiscriminately because they cannot defend one another directly unless they are far apart. Here the winning method is to bring the King up, set up two passed Pawns and at the appropriate

No. 150A

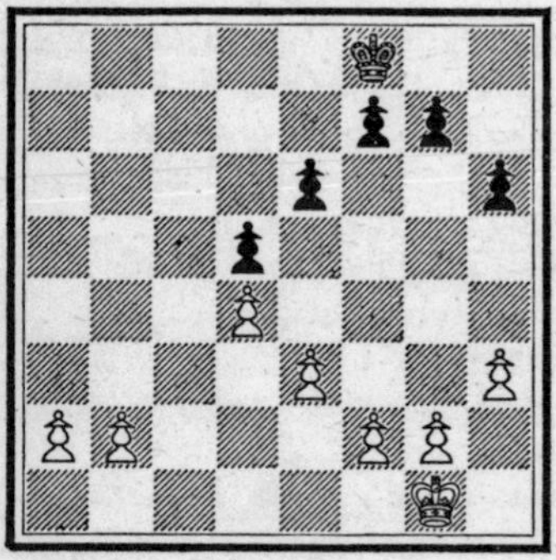

White wins.

No. 150B

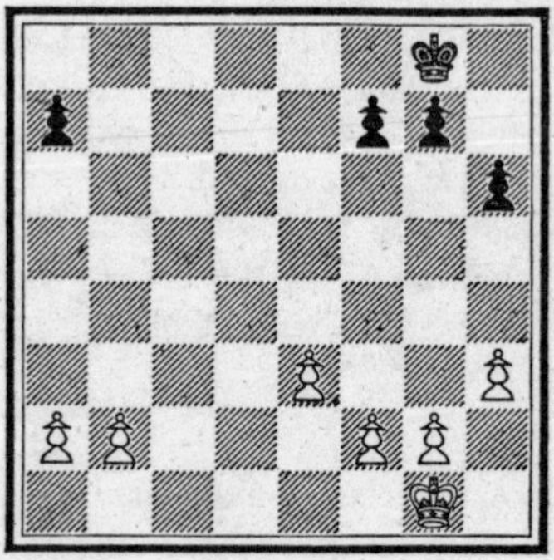

White wins.

No. 151A

White wins.

No. 151B

White wins.

No. 152A

No. 152B

White wins.   White wins.

moment sacrifice one to queen the other. 1 K—B1, K—B1; 2 K—K2, K—K2; 3 K—Q3, K—Q3; 4 K—Q4, K—B3; 5 P—K4, K—Q3; 6 P—B4, P—B3; 7 P—K5ch, P×Pch; 8 P×Pch, K—K3; 9 P—QKt4, K—Q2; 10 P—QR4, K—B3; 11 P—Kt5ch, K—Kt3; 12 P—K6, K—B2; 13 P—R5!, K—Q3; 14 P—Kt6, P×P; 15 P×P, K×P; 16 P—Kt7 and promotes.

Even with only one Pawn to the good, the win rarely involves any complicated combinations. The two most frequent cases are the *outside passed Pawn*, also referred to as the remote or distant passed Pawn (No. 151A) and a two-to-one set-up (No. 151B). The outside passed Pawn is one which is at a distance from the main body of Pawns. The winning idea with it is to use it to deflect the enemy King to one side, and then to penetrate to the other wing with one's own King. Thus in No. 151A White should prepare to divert Black's King to the Q-wing and then go to the K-wing and gobble up the Pawns there. 1 K—B1, K—K2; 2 K—K2, K—Q3; 3 K—Q3, K—B3; 4 K—B3, K—Kt4; 5 K—Kt3, K—R4; 6 P—QR4, K—Kt3 (any Pawn advance would only weaken Black); 7 K—Kt4, K—R3; 8 P—R5, K—Kt2; 9 K—Kt5, K—R2; 10 P—R6, K—Kt1; 11 K—B6, K—R2; 12 K—Q7, K×P; 13 K—K7, K—Kt4; 14 K×P, K—B5; 15 K×KP, P—Kt4; 16 P—Kt4, K—Q6; 17 K×P, K—K7; 18 P—K4 and soon queens.

The two passed Pawns vs. one configuration, reduced to its bare essentials, is shown in No. 151B. Here the winning idea is that the two White Pawns will mutually defend one another and occupy the attention of the Black King. In the meantime White will go over and pick up the Black Pawns. 1 P—QR5, K—Q3; 2 P—Kt5, K—B2; 3 P—R6, K—Kt3; 4 K—B4, K—R2; 5 K—K5, P—Kt4; 6 P×P!

(Note A.), P×P; 7 K—B5, K—Kt3; 8 K×P and the rest has been seen before (No. 122A).

Note A. 6 P—R5?? would be a grave blunder because Black would then have a *protected passed Pawn*, which can never be captured but must always be watched.

The complications which pieces introduce are illustrated in No. 152, where the Pawn positions are essentially unchanged. When the Pawns are connected, the ending is easiest because their continued advance will net a piece sooner or later. No. 152A is relatively difficult because the Pawns are temporarily blocked, but this is soon broken. 1 B—K2, R—R1; 2 R×R, R×R; 3 R—R1, Kt—K5; 4 P—Kt6!, Kt—B6; 5 B—R6, R—R1; 6 P—Kt7, R—Kt1; 7 R—QB1, Kt×P; 8 R—B8 and White will cart away everything but the kitchen sink.

If the Pawns are disconnected, they should not be advanced too hastily because they might become too weak to be defended. Thus in No. 152B the winning procedure is to exchange a few pieces first and, if possible, to secure the open file. 1 K—B1, K—B1; 2 K—K2, K—K2; 3 K—Q2, B—Q2; 4 R×R, R×R; 5 R—QB1! This is typical. Black is confronted with a choice of two evils: exchanging Rooks or yielding the open file. 5.... R×R; 6 K×R, B—Kt4; 7 Kt—B6ch, B×Kt; 8 B×B, K—Q3; 9 B—B3, K—B2; 10 K—Q2, K—Kt3; 11 K—B3, P—QR4; 12 P—QKt4, P×Pch; 13 K×P. Now the winning idea is to utilize the RP as an outside passed Pawn—sacrifice it at the appropriate moment and clean up on the K-side. 13 .... K—R3; 14 P—QR4, K—Kt3; 15 P—R5ch, K—R3; 16 K—B5! (the simplest), K×P; 17 K—Q6, K—Kt5; 18 K—K7, K—B6; 19 K×P, K—Q7; 20 K×KtP, Kt—Q2; 21 K×P, K—K8; 22 P—K4, K×P; 23 P—Q5, P×P; 24 P×P, K—K6; 25 K—Kt7, K—B5; 26 P—R4, K—K4; 27 P—R5 and the steady advance will yield first a piece and then a new Queen.

In all cases, it is essential to *avoid blocking the Pawns*. A good rule to follow is to advance the unopposed Pawn first. E.g., in No. 150B, on 1 P—QR4, P—QR4 blocks the Q-side Pawns, but 1 P—QKt4 will always keep them mobile.

The whole discussion leads to three important practical conclusions:

1. If you have two connected passed Pawns, advance them carefully until the opponent must give up a piece to prevent queening.

2. If you have two disconnected passed Pawns, defend one with the King until they are so far forward that one queens. If there are pieces exchange as many as possible. Once your pieces are well placed, straightforward advancing will be sufficient.

3. With an outside passed Pawn, the winning scheme is to use that Pawn to deflect the enemy King to one side, and then to penetrate to the other wing with one's own King. There two extra Pawns, or one which queens by force, will decide.

With only one Pawn to the good, the principles remain the same, but their application is far more complicated. The basic idea is the

FIFTH RULE: IF YOU ARE ONLY ONE PAWN AHEAD, EXCHANGE PIECES, BUT NOT PAWNS.

The reason for this is that if you are left with only one or two pieces and all the Pawns are on one side, you need at least two Pawns extra to win. Of course, it is always true that once all the pieces are off, the Pawn ending is easily won.

Merely advancing the extra Pawn will as a rule do no good. One must use the Pawn to break through with pieces or the King and gain more material.

Another helpful point in such endings is that the most difficult to win are those with Bishops of opposite colors. Endings with Queens also present more problems than those with other pieces.

The fifth rule contains a useful hint for the defense: to swap Pawns, but not pieces.

No. 153

White wins.

Positionally, there are a number of considerations which are well worth emphasis.

Mobility of the pieces remains an important consideration in the ending. Centralization and preservation of freedom of action are good strategy at all times.

There are a few good pointers to remember about each piece.

The *Bishop* needs wide and open diagonals; the worst thing in the world that can happen to it is to be shut in behind a mass of Pawns. An example of what ensues in that event is No. 153. If it were Black's move, he would have to give up a Pawn at once, for the B is defending both QP and KRP, and the King is preventing his rival from coming in. But White to play can easily gain a tempo because he has far more room for his Bishop: 1 B—Q2, B—Kt2; 2 B—B1!, B—B1; 3 B—B4 and Black is lost. A likely continuation is 3 .... B—K2; 4 B×RP, B—Q1; 5 B—Kt7, B—K2; 6 P—R6 and queens. To avoid straitjackets of this type we have our

SIXTH RULE: DO NOT PLACE YOUR PAWNS ON THE SAME COLOR AS YOUR BISHOP.

We have already seen (p. 91) that the Bishop is ordinarily slightly more mobile than the Knight. In the ending this superior speed is of much greater consequence than in the middle game, which gives us our

SEVENTH RULE: A BISHOP IS BETTER THAN A KNIGHT IN ALL BUT BLOCKED PAWN POSITIONS.

It must not be supposed that a Bishop is so much stronger that it can nullify a Pawn plus, or that it should win with even Pawns. With a Pawn to the good the ending is theoretically won regardless of which piece one has, while with even Pawns one cannot win unless there is some other advantage. Nevertheless, the superiority, though not as great as a Pawn, is quite real.

A striking example of the power of the Bishop is seen in No. 154A. After 1 .... B—R3ch! White had to give way to one side or the other and allow Black to penetrate to his Pawns. The game con-

No. 154A

Black to play wins.

No. 154B

Black wins.

tinued 2 K—B3 (Note A.), P—R3; 3 Kt—Q4, P—Kt3; 4 Kt—B2, K—K5; 5 Kt—K3, P—B4; 6 K—Q2, P—B5; 7 Kt—Kt4, P—R4; 8 Kt—B6ch, K—B4; 9 Kt—Q7, B—B1; 10 Kt—B8, P—Kt4; 11 P—Kt3 (Note B.), P×RP; 12 P×RP, K—Kt5; 13 Kt—Kt6, B—B4; 14 Kt—K7, B—K3; 15 P—Kt4, K×P; 16 K—Q3, K—Kt5; 17 K—K4, P—R5; 18 Kt—B6, B—B4ch; 19 K—Q5, P—B6; 20 P—Kt5, P—R6; 21 Kt×P, P—R7; 22 P—Kt6, P—R8=Q and the rest is simple.

Note A. If 2 K—K3, K—B4; 3 Kt—K5, K—Kt5; 4 Kt×P, K×P; 5 Kt—K5, B—Kt4; 6 P—B4, P—QR4; and the Black QRP cannot be stopped.

Note B. On 11 P×P, K×P; 12 P—B3, K—B3! White's Kt is stalemated and will soon be lost.

The type position where the Bishop is bad is No. 154B. No less than four Pawns are fixed on Black, while White has only one legal Pawn move. In such blocked or close positions the Bishop is useless. Black won as follows: 1 .... Kt—Kt4; 2 B—Q2, Kt—R6; 3 B—B1 (Note A.), Kt—Kt8; 4 B—Kt2, P—R6!; 5 B—R1, K—Q3! (to gain a move; a maneuver known as triangulation); 6 K—K2, K—B3; 7 K—Q1 (Note B.), K—Q4; 8 K—B2, K—K5; 9 K×Kt, K—B6; 10 B—Kt2, P×B; 11 P—R4, K×P; 12 P—R5, K—R7; 13 P—R6, P—Kt6; 14 P—R7, P—Kt7; 15 P—R8=Q, P—Kt8=Qch; 16 K×P, Q—Kt7ch; 17 Q×Qch, K×Q; 18 K—R3, K—B6; 19 K—Kt4, K×P; 20 K×P, K—K6; 21 P—Q5, P×Pch; 22 K×P, P—B5 and Black queens by force, when the rest is easy: 23 P—B4, P—B6; 24 P—B5, P—B7; 25 P—B6, P—B8=Q; 26 P—B7, Q—B4ch; 27 K—B6, Q—QB1! Now the Black Queen remains at QB1 until the Black King can come up and capture the Pawn.

Note A. If 3 B—K1, Kt—Kt8; 4 B—Q2, Kt×B; 5 K×Kt, K—K5; 6 K—K2, P—R6. Now Black has the *opposition*, because of which White must give way to one side or the other. E.g., 7 K—Q2, K—B6; 8 K—K1, K×P; 9 K—B1, K—R7 followed by queening the KtP.

Note B. If 7 K—K3, K—Q4; 8 K—B2, K—K5; 9 K—K2, Kt—Q7!!; 10 K×Kt, K—B6; 11 K—K1, K×P and despite the fact that he is a piece ahead White cannot prevent the KtP from queening. An amusing illustration of the uselessness of an immobilized piece!

With Rooks there are three important points to remember. All are based on the fact that a Rook should not be hemmed in by Pawns.

In the first place, *open files should be seized by the Rooks*. This is also true of the middle game, but is usually more important in the ending. Now, the object of getting on an open file is to penetrate to the enemy lines, and this invasion is most effective when the Rook gets to the seventh rank. As a matter of fact, such a Rook is so strong that we have the

EIGHTH RULE: IT IS WORTH GIVING UP A PAWN TO GET A ROOK ON THE SEVENTH RANK.

This rule, it must be added, holds only when there are a number of Pawns on each side (five or more) and when these Pawns are on their own second rank, i.e., not so far advanced that the enemy Rook is just growling at thin air.

An example of the effectiveness of such a Rook is No. 155. Black is a Pawn behind. If he tries to save the second Pawn by 1 .... R—QKt1?; 2 P—QR4 will leave his Rook wholly passive. Instead he drew by 1 .... R—Q7!!, with the continuation 2 R×Pch, K—Kt4; 3 K—K1, R—B7; 4 R—Kt5, K—Kt5; 5 P—R3ch (Note A.), K×P, 6 R×P, R×KtP; 7 R—B4, R×RP; 8 R×P, P—R4! (see third rule); 9 P—QB4, K—Kt7!; 10 R—KB4, R—QB7; 11 R—KR4, K—B6;

12 K—Q1, R×KBP; 13 P—B5, K—K6; 14 R×P, K—Q5 and a draw was agreed to.

Note A.   If 5 P—QR4, P—B5; 6 P—R5, K—B6; 7 K—Q1, R×BP; 8 P—R6, P—K6; 9 P—R7, R—B8ch; 10 K—B2, R—QR8 and Black will win.

With fewer Pawns on the board, a basic principle is our

No. 155

Black to play draws.

NINTH RULE: ROOKS BELONG BEHIND PASSED PAWNS.

The reason is that this is the only way a Rook can retain its mobility.

A striking verification of the rule is seen in No. 156.   In 156A White's Rook is in front of the Pawn and has no move which does not leave the P en prise, while Black's Rook is behind it and has miles of leeway.   It will do White no good to bring his King up to the Pawn because he will only be checked away.   E.g., 1 K—B3, R—R6ch; 2 K—K4, R—R8; 3 K—Q5, R—R7; 4 K—B6, R—R8; 5 K—Kt7,

No. 156A

Draw.

No. 156B

White wins.

R—Kt8ch; 6 K—R6, R—R8ch; 7 K—Kt6, R—Kt8ch; 8 K—B5, R—QR8 etc.

But in 156B the roles are reversed.   Here Black's Rook is tied down and becomes a useless chunk of wood, while White's is mobile. As a result, the White King can force a decision by penetrating to one side or the other.   1 K—B3, K—B3; 2 K—K4, K—K3; 3 R—R6ch, K—Q2; 4 K—Q5, K—B2 (if he goes to the other side White's King goes to the support of the QRP and wins a Rook); 5 K—K5, K—Kt2; 6 R—R2, R—K1ch; 7 K—B6, K—R1; 8 K×P, R—K5; 9 K—Kt7, R—K2ch; 10 K—R6, R—KB2; 11 P—B4, R—K2; 12 P—Kt4, R—KB2; 13 P—Kt5!, R—K2; 14 R—R6, R—KB2; 15 R—KB6, R—B2; 16 R—B8ch, K×P; 17 R—KR8, R—B5; 18 R×Pch, K—Kt3; 19 R—KB7, R—B7; 20 K×P, R×P; 21 P—B5 and the two Pawns decide quickly by advancing.

The defender in an ending must pin all his hopes on a counterattack.   He must try to set up passed Pawns of his own, he must see to it that his pieces are not tied down.   But when the enemy, as is usually the case, also has a passed Pawn he is always compelled to see to it that that Pawn does not get out of bounds.   Technically, he must stop or blockade the passed Pawn.   The only two pieces which do not lose any of their mobility when blockading are the King and the Knight.   If there is a choice between a Knight and a Bishop as blockaders, the Knight should be chosen.   But in general the best blockader is the King because he is least able to undertake a counteraction in some other part of the board.   Thus gives us our

TENTH RULE: BLOCKADE PASSED PAWNS WITH THE KING.

No. 157 is an illustration of the value of this rule.

No. 157A

No. 157B

Draw.   White wins.

In 157A the QKtP is blockaded by the King and the game is drawn. It is out of the question to drive the Black King away from QKt2, so White must try 1 K—K7, B—Kt5; 2 K—B6, K—B3; 3 K—Kt7, B—R4; 4 K×P, K—Kt2, when, although he has won a Pawn, he is blocked on all sides. As long as he stays at KKt7 or KR7 Black plays his King back and forth, but once he switches to the Q-side Black gets his King to Kt2 and plays his B back and forth.

The difference in blockading force is at once apparent by comparison with No. 157B. Here the B will die a gallant death in short order: 1 K—B7, B—B6; 2 P—Kt7, B×P; 3 K×B. The rest is simple: White goes to the K-side and captures at least one Pawn there.

PROBLEMS

No. 61

White to play and draw.

No. 62

White to play and win.

No. 63

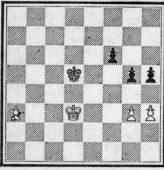

White to play and win.

No. 64

White to play. Who wins?

No. 65

White to play and win.

No. 66

Why does White have the better position? How can he win?

No. 67

White to play and win.

No. 68

Black to play. Who has the better position and how should he continue?

No. 69

White to play and draw.

No. 70

White to play and win.

No. 71

No. 72

White to play and win.

Black to play and draw.

SOLUTIONS TO PROBLEMS

Chapter II

No. 1. 1 Q—Kt3, K—R3; 2 Q—Kt6 mate.

No. 2. 1 Q—K7! (stalemate must be avoided), K—Kt1; 2 K—Kt6, K—R1; 3 Q—Kt7 mate.

No. 3. 1 Q—K4, K—Q2; 2 Q—K5, K—Q1; 3 K—B6, K—B1; 4 Q—K8 mate.

No. 4. 1 K—B6, K—B1; 2 R—K8 mate.

No. 5. 1 Kt—K7! (watch out for stalemate!), K—R2; 2 Kt—B8ch, K—R1; 3 B—B3 mate.

No. 6. 1 Kt—K4!—keeping the Black King confined. 1 K—B5 is fair, but any other move is weak.

Chapter IV

No. 7. Bad. The Bishop attacks nothing and will be driven away with loss of time. Best is 2 .... Kt—KB3; 3 Kt—QB3, P—B3; 4 B—R4, B—B4 and Black is somewhat better developed.

No. 8. 3 .... P—Q4, to gain the upper hand in the center. It may be postponed one or two moves, but must occur sooner or later.

No. 9. First, second and eighth. Proceed against it by normal development.

No. 10. Black. He has undisputed control of Q5, while any White piece that plays to his Q4 can be chased away by .... P—QB3.

No. 11. Black. His development is superior. The White Queen has been brought out too early.

No. 12. No. He has gained only one tempo for it.

Chapter V

No. 13. Bad because it weakens the King position and deprives the KKt of its most natural square. 4 B—QB4 followed by speedy natural development is the best procedure.

No. 14. It does not develop a piece and has no effect on the center. 5 P—Q4, P×P; 6 P×P, B—Kt3; 7 O—O gives White an ideal set-up.

No. 15. 6 .... Kt×KP. Always get rid of an enemy center Pawn.

No. 16.   The only good reply is 11 .... P—KB4.   The trap is 11 .... Kt(B5)—Q3?; 12 Q×KtP, Q—B3; 13 Q×Q, Kt×Q; 14 R—K1ch, K—B1; 15 B—R6ch, K—Kt1; 16 R—K5, Kt(B3)—K5; 17 R—K1, P—KB4; 18 R—K7, P—Kt3; 19 Kt—R4, B—Kt2; 20 R—Kt7ch, K—B1; 21 R×RP dis ch, K—Kt1; 22 R—Kt7ch, K—B1; 23 Kt—Kt6ch and wins.

No. 17.   Both 4 P—B3 and 4 O—O are excellent: White should plan to set up a strong Pawn center at an early stage.   A sample continuation is 4 P—B3, KKt—K2; 5 P—Q4, P×P; 6 P×P, B—Kt5ch; 7 B—Q2, B×Bch; 8 Q×B, P—QR3; 9 B—R4, with advantage to White.

No. 18.   11 .... Q—Q2? loses a piece after 12 Kt×B!   If then 12 .... P×Kt; 13 R×Kt!, and if 12 .... Q×Kt; 13 R×Kt!, for the Black QP is pinned in both cases.

The Black QKt must move.   On 11 .... Kt×Kt; 12 P×Kt time must be lost to extricate the Kt at K5.

11 .... Kt×KP is considered best because it gives Black a strong counter-attack after 12 P—B3, B—Q3!; 13 P×Kt, B—KKt5; 14 Q—B2, P—QB4.

No. 19.   9 Kt—Q5, to break up the Black King position.

No. 20.   Black wishes to give back the Pawn and secure a better ending rather than try to hold on to the extra material at the expense of a cramped position.   The main variation is 8 P×P, P×P; 9 Q×Qch, Kt×Q; 10 Kt×P, B—K3.

No. 21.   3 .... P—QB4.   In such positions it is imperative to break up the White center Pawn formation.

No. 22.   P—QB4!   This prevents both any eventual counterplay on the QB file and the advance of the Black QP.

No. 23.   It does nothing about the center and violates the rule that Knights should be developed before Bishops.   The best answer is 3 .... P×P; 4 P—K3, P—QKt4, when White has insufficient compensation for the Pawn.

No. 24.   3 P×P, to secure the better Pawn center after 3 .... Kt×P; 4 P—K4.   After 3 .... Q×P; 4 Kt—QB3 Black will likewise be at a disadvantage because he has no Pawn in the center.

Chapter VI

No. 25.   The best plan is to exchange all the pieces except one White Rook and the Black Knight.   This can be effected by 1 Q×Q, Kt×Q (Note A.); 2 P×P, R×P (Note B.); 3 B—R3, R—B3; 4 B×Bch, R×B (Note C.); 5 R×R, Kt×R.   Now 6 R—Kt1! followed by King entry is the quickest way to win.

Note A.   If 1 .... P×Q; 2 P×P, B×KBP; 3 R×Kt wins.

Note B.   2 .... B×KBP leaves the KP en prise.

Note C. Or 4 .... Kt×B; 5 P—B5, again winning the KP.

No. 26. To exploit the less mobile Black position by beginning an attack against the King. The strongest execution of this plan is R—R3, to concentrate forces on the KKt file.

No. 27. He must plan to attack on the KKt file. With this in mind O—O—O is the most forceful continuation.

No. 28. Black. White should try to build up an attack on the open KR file, while Black should exchange Queens and concentrate on the weak White Pawns.

No. 29. Black. He is in effect a Pawn ahead, since the three White Pawns on the Q-side are held by his two (no passed Pawn can be created). In addition his King position has been weakened.

No. 30. 1 P—KB4.

No. 31. 1 P—Kt5, Kt—Q3 (Note A.); 2 P×P, Kt—B1; 3 P—Q6, Kt—R2; 4 P—Q7, Kt—B3; 5 P—R7 and one Pawn will queen.

Note A. This is the only way to stop the RP from queening. If 1 .... Kt×P; 2 P×P and the Kt cannot get back.

No. 32. 1 B—B6.

No. 33. 1 B×Pch and 2 B×R.

No. 34. 1 B—B3 and if 1 .... Kt—Q5 or 1 .... Kt—K4, 2 B×Kt.

No. 35. 1 R—Q1. Any B move but 1 .... B—Kt4 allows mate, while 1 .... B—Kt4 is refuted by 2 P×B.

No. 36. 1 R—B1ch, K—K3; 2 R×B.

No. 37. 1 R—R3.

No. 38. 1 Kt—B5. 1 Kt—Q4?, R—Kt2 is not so good.

No. 39. 1 Kt—B7ch.

No. 40. 1 Q—R6. 1 Q—Kt5 is good, but not quite so conclusive.

No. 41. 1 Q—Q1, and if 1 .... Q—B2; 2 Q—R5ch and mate next.

No. 42. 1 R—K1, Q—K2; 2 P—KB3.

No. 43. 1 Q—B5, P—KKt3 (the only move to stop mate); 2 Q×B.

No. 44. 1 Kt—Q6 dis ch.

No. 45. 1 Kt—K5 dis ch, K—Kt1; 2 Kt—Q7.

No. 46. 1 B×Pch, K×B; 2 Kt—Kt5ch, K—Kt3 (Note A.); 3 Q—Kt4, P—B4; 4 Q—Kt3, R—R1; 5 Kt×P dis ch, K—B2; 6 Kt×Qch etc.

Note A. If 2 .... K—Kt1; 3 Q—R5, R—K1; 4 Q—R7ch, K—B1; 5 Q×P mate, while if 2 .... K—R3; 3 Q—Kt4, R—R1; 4 Kt×Pch, K—R2; 5 Q×P mate.

No. 47. By 1 B—R6, followed by P—KR4, P—KKt4 and P—KR5, opening the KR file.

No. 48. On the principle that in cramped positions you free yourself by exchanging, the best defensive plan involves the immediate exchange of two minor pieces by releasing the pin: 1 .... P×P;

2 B×P, Kt—Q4; 3 B×B, Q×B; 4 O—O, Kt×Kt etc. To continue the liberation of his game Black should then play .... P—K4.

Chapter VII

No. 49.   1 .... K—Q3 and if 2 K—K4, K—K3, etc., retaining the opposition.

No. 50.   1 K—Kt4!, K—B3; 2 K—B4, K—Q3; 3 K—Q4, K—K3; 4 K—K4, K—B3; 5 K—B4, K—K3; 6 K—Kt5 etc. as in No. 120. 1 K—B4?, K—B3; 2 K—Q4, K—Q3 etc. only draws.

No. 51.   1 P—Kt7, K—R2; 2 P—Kt8=Qch! (Note A.), K×Q; 3 K—Kt6, K—R1; 4 K—B7, K—R2; 5 P—Kt6 ch etc.

Note A.   But not 2 P—Kt6ch??, K—Kt1, or 2 K—B7??, stalemate.

No. 52.   1 Kt—Q3! followed by playing the K over to the Q-side.

No. 53.   Draw. Black's King is too near the Pawns.

No. 54.   1 B—Kt5! (to stalemate the Kt), K—K4; 2 K—Q3, K—B3; 3 K—Q4, K—K2; 4 P—K5, K—B2; 5 K—Q5, etc. Any other first move would allow the Kt to get to K4, blockading the Pawns and drawing.

No. 55.   1 K—B5!, K—K2; 2 K—Kt6, K—B1; 3 B—B4, B—Q5; 4 P—KR5, K—K2; 5 P—R6, B—Kt7; 6 P—R7, B—B6; 7 P—R5!, K—Q2; 8 P—R6, K—B2; 9 K—B7, K—Kt3; 10 K—Kt8, K—R2; 11 P—R8=Q, B×Q; 12 K×B etc. The Black King must not be allowed to get to KR1, since he will then give up his B for the QRP and draw against RP+B of the wrong color.

No. 56.   1 K—K3, P—R6; 2 K—B2, K— R5; 3 R—Kt4, K—Kt4; 4 K—Kt3, K—R4; 5 R—Kt5ch, K—Kt3; 6 K×P, P—R7; 7 R—Kt1 etc.

No. 57.   1 P—Kt5! gives No. 137. White must not lose any time, since 1 K—R4?, R—R1ch; 2 K—Kt5, R—Kt1ch; 3 K—R4, R—R1ch; 4 K—Kt3, R—KKt1 only draws.

No. 58.   1 K—B6!, R—KKt8; 2 R—R4ch!, K×P; 3 P—Kt5, R—Kt3ch; 4 K—Kt7, R—Kt2ch; 5 K—R6, R—Kt3ch; 6 P—Kt6, R—K3; 7 K—R7 and the Rook will soon have to be sacrificed for the Pawn.

No. 59.   1 Q—Kt5ch, K—B7; 2 Q—R4ch, K—Kt7; 3 Q—Kt4ch, K—R7; 4 K—B3, K—R8; 5 Q×Pch etc. Black to play moves 1 .... P—R7 and draws (141C).

No. 60.   1 Q—Q8ch and 2 Q×R. Continue the ending with Q vs. B. It is easier to mate with Q vs. B than with Q vs. R. The procedure is essentially the same as that in No. 144.

Chapter VIII

No. 61.   1 P—K5, Kt—B5ch; 2 K—K4, forcing the exchange of Black's last Pawn.

No. 62. 1 P—R5, R—R1; 2 P—R6, K—B1; 3 P—Kt5, K—K2; 4 P—Kt6, K—Q2; 5 P—Kt7, R—K1; 6 P—R7 and queens.

No. 63. 1 P—Kt4!, P×P; 2 P×P, K—B4; 3 K—K4, K—Kt4; 4 K—B5, K—R5; 5 K×P, K×P; 6 K×P etc. Note that 1 P—QR4, P—B4 is not quite sufficient: 2 P—R5, K—B4; 3 P—R6, K—Kt3; 4 K—Q4, K×P; 5 K—K5, P—R5!; 6 P×P, P×P; 7 K×P, K—Kt2; 8 K—Kt4, K—B1; 9 K×P, K—Q2; 10 K—Kt5, K—K2; 11 K—Kt6, K—B1 and draws.

No. 64. White. Black cannot hold both Pawns and cannot push his own fast enough. Thus: 1 P—KR4, P—Q4; 2 P—R5, K—K2; 3 P—R4, P—K4; 4 P—R5, P—K5ch; 5 K—Q4, K—B3; 6 P—QR6 etc.

No. 65. 1 P—QKt4, K—Q3; 2 P—QR4, K—B3; 3 P—Kt5ch, P×P; 4 BP×Pch, K—B4; 5 P—Kt4, P×P; 6 P×P, K—Kt3; 7 K—Q5, K—Kt2; 8 K—K6 and after cleaning up the K-side White will return to the other wing.

No. 66. Because three of Black's Pawns are on White, giving him a bad Bishop. 1 B—Kt2, B—Q2; 2 B—R1!, B—K1; 3 B—B3, B—Q2; 4 B×RP, B—K3; 5 B—K8, B×P; 6 B×P, B—Kt6; 7 B—Kt7!, B×P; 8 P—B6, K—Kt3; 9 P—B7, B—Q2; 10 P—B8=Q, B×Q; 11 B×B, P—R5; 12 B—K6, P—R6; 13 K—Kt3, K—B3; 14 B—R2, K—K2; 15 K—B3, K—Q3; 16 K—K3, K—B4; 17 K—Q3, K—Kt5; 18 K—Q4, K—Kt4; 19 K—K5 etc.

No. 67. 1 P—R6, B—Q4; 2 P—R7, B—B3; 3 B—B4, K—K2; 4 B—Q5.

No. 68. White stands much better because the Pawn position is blocked. 1 Kt—Q3, B—B4; 2 Kt—B4, B—Kt5; 3 P—QKt4! wins a Pawn.

No. 69. 1 R—Q8ch, K—Kt2; 2 R—QR8, R×RP; 3 R—R6 draws because the Black King cannot go over to the Q-wing without giving up too many Pawns. 1 R—QR1?, K—Kt2; 2 K—B3, K—B3 would lose for White.

No. 70. 1 P—R5, R—R1; 2 R—QR4, R—R3; 3 K—B3, K—B1; 4 K—K4, K—K2; 5 K—Q5, K—Q2; 6 K—B5, K—B2; 7 K—Kt5, K—Kt2; 8 R—K4 followed by mopping up on the K-side.

No. 71. 1 P—QR4, K—B3; 2 P—R5, R—B8ch; 3 K—R2, R—QR8; 4 P—QKt4, P—K4; 5 R—Kt6ch, K—B4; 6 P—R6, P—K5; 7 P—Kt5, R—R7; 8 R—Kt7, K—K3; 9 P—R7, P—B4; 10 P—Kt6, P—B5; 11 R—Kt8 etc.

No. 72. 1 .... K—B2; 2 K—K3, K—K3; 3 K—Q4, K—Q2; 4 K—B5, B—Kt4; 5 K—Kt6, K—B1; 6 P—R4, B×P; 7 K×P, B—B3; 8 K—Kt6, B—B6; 9 K—B5. Now Black will keep his King at QKt2 and White can at best win one Pawn on the K-side (the KKtP) but will never be able to force a passed Pawn there.

GLOSSARY OF TERMS COMMONLY USED IN CHESS LITERATURE

EN PRISE means capturable. Literally, it is French for "in take."

The *EXCHANGE* is a Rook for a minor piece. Winning the exchange is winning a Rook for a Knight or a Bishop.

FORCE is the number of men. If one player has more and better men he is ahead in force.

A *FORK* is a simultaneous attack on two pieces by a single unit.

A *GAMBIT* is an opening in which some material is sacrificed, usually for the sake of an attack.

A *MAN* is any unit.

MATERIAL is the same as force.

MOBILITY is freedom of action.

A *PIECE* is a Knight, Bishop, Rook or Queen. A *MINOR PIECE* is either a Knight or a Bishop. The *HEAVY PIECES* are the Queens and Rooks.

A *PIN* occurs when a man screens a unit of higher value.

SPACE is the number of squares covered. The player who controls forty (or any other number greater than 32) of the sixty-four squares has more space.

SYMBOLS frequently seen are:

!	excellent move
?	weak move
=	even position
∓	Black has the better game
±	White has the better game

A *TEMPO* is the unit of time—it is the same as one move. To gain a tempo is to gain a move, i.e., to do in two moves what ordinarily would require three, or in three what would usually take four.

TIME is the number of moves. If one player has made more moves and has used them to good purpose he is ahead in time.

ZUGZWANG is a position where there is no direct threat, but any move made leads to a loss. Literally, German for "move forced."

INDEX

F. REINFELD, Keres' Best Games

F. REINFELD AND I. CHERNEV, Chess Strategy and Tactics

F. REINFELD AND R. FINE, Dr. Lasker's Chess Career

R. RETI, Masters of the Chessboard

P. W. SERGEANT, Morphy's Games of Chess

P. W. SERGEANT AND W. WATTS, Pillsbury's Chess Career

TOURNAMENT BOOKS

Practically every important tournament ever played has had a book devoted to it. The most worth while ones in English are:

Hastings, 1895. Annotations by the competitors.

Hastings, 1922. Annotations by DR. A. ALEKHINE.

New York, 1924. Annotations by DR. A. ALEKHINE.

Warsaw, 1935. Annotations by F. REINFELD.

Semmering-Baden, 1937. Annotations by F. REINFELD.

MAGAZINES

The leading periodicals in English are:

Australasian Chess Magazine. Edited by C. S. PURDY. Sidney.

Chess Life. Edited by U.S. Chess Federation, N.Y.

British Chess Magazine. Edited by J. DU MONT. London.

Chess. Edited by B. H. WOOD. Sutton Coldfield, England.

Chess Review. Edited by I. A. HOROWITZ. New York.

INDEX